RECOVERY
RULES

100 TRUISMS THAT WILL CHANGE
EVERYTHING

MARK DENISON, D.MIN.

*"This collection of 100 recovery rules is destined to
become a touchstone for the recovery community."*
Michael, Leahy, BraveHearts

Austin Brothers
— PUBLISHING —
www.abpbooks.com

ENDORSEMENTS

"You need this book if you are serious about recovery. Dr. Denison unlocks often overlooked simple, but profound truths that can make the difference between successful recovery and mediocre recovery. Once again, he brings hope to those who have been beaten down by addiction. This is a book of hope, healing, and good health. It will make a difference in the lives of many men, women, and couples. Thanks for sharing this with the recovery community!"

Dr. Milton S. Magness, MA Psy, MA, LPC, CSAT
Founder, Hope & Freedom
Author, *Real Hope, True Freedom*
HopeAndFreedom.com

"Mark's 'Recovery Rules' is an honest, hard-hitting, and hopeful guide down the path of any recovery journey. Mark has poured out biblical wisdom mixed with practical application from his own personal recovery and countless hours of ministering and helping others do the same. Whether you are in a recovery program, looking for healthy ways to process your pain, or helping others who are, this book is a timeless resource of inspiration and insight."

Ed Young
Founding Pastor, Fellowship Church, Grapevine, Texas
Bestselling author, New York Times

"Powerful, insightful, and fun. The road to recovery needs a daily jolt, and 'Recovery Rules' is it! Mark Denison delivers memorable slices of wisdom that you can't help but chew on and come back for more."

Sam Black
Covenant Eyes, Director of Recovery Education
Author, *The Healing Church: What Churches Get Wrong About Pornography and How to Fix It*

"These 100 recovery rules will help you walk out the journey of recovery with integrity. I encourage you to implement each one of them!"

Tom Weaver
Founder, Come to the Table Ministry, TableMinistry.com

"A remarkable achievement. Mark Denison has created a simple, yet highly effective resource that is truly reader-friendly. Written from the heart and infused with his own experience, Denison's book of recovery rules is a resource that speaks to individuals in any phase of their recovery journey."

Erin Grupp, LCSW, CAP, CST, CSAT
Founder, Catalyst Center for Change
info@catalyshelp.com

"Direct, humorous, and skillfully subtle – this book has it all! Mark has put pen to paper for the creation of a relevant and practical manual for upgrading anyone's recovery. It's simple enough for anyone to read it, and meaningful enough for anyone to learn from it."

Dr. Jake Porter
Founder and President, Daring Ventures
DaringVentures.com

"An expert in addiction, Mark has given us the instruction manual that will help you break the ugly cycle of addiction. These 100 practical and inspiring rules offer a comprehensive set of tools to push your addiction to the past."

Clair Hoover
Executive Director, National Coalition of Men's Ministries
Ncmm.org

"Recovery, restoration, redemption, reconciliation, renewal, relationships. Each of these are at the heart of God's message to those who have been crushed and demoralized by addiction. God's Word offers freedom. Mark's 'Recovery Rules' are practical, quick-hitting truths to keep you on the right track. This is the perfect tool to take you further, deeper, and higher."

Rod Handley
Founder and President, Character that Counts
CharacterThatCounts.org

"I absolutely love what Mark has done here. The recovery community is famous for its pointed truths, stated as memorable turns of phrase. These simple rules of recovery could be called rules for living! Read them and live by them. You will be glad you did."

Dr. James M. Reeves
Author, *Refuge*
Producer, Fearless Series for Women, Fearless Series for Man

"This book brings humor and common sense to a serious and complex subject, and injects the reader with recovery knowledge passed down through the ages. A great read for anyone in any recovery group!"

Jorge L. Sesin
Founder, Castimonia
Castimonia.org

"Prepare to be challenged, to laugh, and even cry as you read these rules of recovery. They will help you get over the hump and be the person you were created to be."

Mike Rosas
Chaplain, Houston Rockets
Evangelist, author, Story Tellers
HolySociety.org

"In this book, you will find life-altering statements that will deposit investments in your personal growth. Mark's Rules will motivate and inspire you!"

Guy Earle
Co-Founder, Think Twice Ministries
ThinkTwiceMinistries.org

"I love Mark's no-nonsense approach. This guide will pull you out of the ditch. It cuts through the noise. I highly recommend it to anyone on the road to recovery."

Vern Tompke
Podcast Host, Finding Traction and Pastors on Porn

"With insightful truisms that offer strength and hope, Mark Denison's 'Recovery Rules' provides empowering daily guidance for anyone seeking to walk the road of recovery and healing. This encouraging collection of 100 thoughtful rules is destined to become a touchstone for the recovery community."

Michael Leahy
Founder, BraveHearts
Bravehearts.org

"Mark Denison's 'Recovery Rules' are a great tool for anyone seeking recovery from addiction. This book is easy to understand, practical to use, and a great source of hope."

Robert Posner
Founder, 24:16 Recovery
2416ministries.org

"Mark has done it again, with wit, wisdom, and practicality. These 'Recovery Rules' are simple, yet effective. Mark combines years of sobriety and experience in giving us the tools needed to stay sober and to heal."

Steve O'Connor
Founder, Mercyfy Recovery
Mercyfy.com

"This is full of recovery wisdom for people living in the trenches of addiction. If you want impactful antidotes that will empower you for daily living, this is it!"

Thomas Kenyan
Real Life Coaching

"Everyone needs practical wisdom to navigate the rough waters of recovery. 'Recovery Rules' give you time-tested guidelines to make it all the way home."

Dr. Ben Young
Teaching Pastor, Second Baptist Church, Houston, Texas
Author, *Survive the Day*

"I have celebrated the many ways God has used Mark over the 30-plus years of our friendship. His expertise and attention to detail make this a must-have recovery tool. I give it my highest recommendation!"

Steve Long, MS
Licensed Professional Counselor

"This book is a powerful resource of encouragement for anyone coping with addictions. It is a must-read for living! I highly recommend 'Recovery Rules' to everyone, whether in recovery or just living the human experience!"

Elmo Winters
Founder, Kingdom Group KingdomGroup.com

"Mark's depth of experience in the field of recovery makes this a must-read for anyone in recovery. Put these rules into practice and you will be on your way to success. I will recommend this book to all my fellow purity warriors and program leaders."

Dave Howe
Founder, Live Pure Ministries
Author, *Live Pure and Free – The 90-Day Game Changer*
DaveHowe.org

"I endorse Mark's latest work, both as a colleague and dear friend. His authority on recovery shines through, offering practical insights and actionable strategies that provide a guiding light for those seeking transformation and healing."

Ray Dick
Care Pastor, Grace Community Church
Sarasota, Florida

"This amazing book is infused with hard-won wisdom, lived experience and wise counsel. These daily reminders will equip you to thrive in your recovery and walk in freedom. 'Recovery Rules' is profound."

Ervin Lee
Founder, From Beer to the Bible
Frombeertothebible.com

"This book provides practical, real-life application, addressing spiritual and emotional aspects of recovery. My friend and colleague has given us a comprehensive approach packed with incredible gems. By reading just one rule each day, you will chart a new path."

Tim Groves, PSAP
Professional Life Coach

"Mark Denison's 'Recovery Rules' is a strategically useful book for everyone who wants to live the life we were meant to live. This book is filled with information, insights, and practical points which will enable every reader to grow in their recovery, whether they're beginning the journey or are well along the road."

T.C. Ryan, DMin, PSAP-S
Executive Director, Living Integrated
Author, *Ashamed No More: A Pastor's Journey Through Sex Addiction*

"Mark Denison has given us a wonderful, practical resource that creates a mindset of living one day at a time. This book will help you find the grace and wisdom to face life's greatest challenges and live in the present."

Rodney Wright
Pure Desire Ministries
Author, *How to Talk to Your Kids About Sex*

Recovery Rules
Mark Denison D.Min.

ISBN: 979-8-9867751-4-2

Cover design by Laurie Barboza - Design Stash Books

(DesignStashBooks@gmail.com)

Printed in the United States of America
2023 -- First Edition

Published by Austin Brothers Publishing

Austin Brothers
— PUBLISHING —
www.abpbooks.com

I dedicate this work to my dear friend Steve.
You have been my friend,
my sponsor, and my encourager.

I have watched you do recovery
better than anyone I know.

I am grateful for your support
and for your silent contribution to this project.

Contents

INTRODUCTION

The recovery community has produced hundreds of helpful sayings. Many of us have committed dozens of them to memory. I cherish any helpful truism, regardless of the source. And I love to read recovery material. In doing so, over the years of my recovery, I have jotted down a few of my own nuggets. At first, there was just one.

If you're 90 percent in, you're 100 percent out.

I don't know when or how that came to me. It just made sense. A lot of sense. I found myself saying that – a lot. Ask any of the men I have sponsored across the years, and they can vouch for that. Ask any of the 200 men who have been in my Freedom Groups. They are probably sick of hearing it. But it's true. So I say it a lot. And then another truism came to me one day.

Addiction isn't a bad problem; it's a bad solution.

Think about that for a second. We spend years trying to quit the problem, when it was never a problem in the first place, as much as it was a solution. Until we dig deeper and ask why we do what we do, the behavior will keep coming back. Then another thought came to me.

Until you take ownership for your disease, you won't take responsibility for your recovery.

And it was on. Every time I thought of something like that, I'd put it in my phone. That has given me the chance to look back at these simple statements whenever I really need them. I wrote them for one person – me. But pretty soon, these three nuggets became 10, then 20, 30, and more. So over the past eight years, it turns out I was writing a book, and didn't even know it. It turns out this was my first book on recovery. I published 10 other recovery books first, but God was at work with this one the whole time. So in a sense, this took me eight years to write. Every time I added another nugget to my list, I was working on a book I never thought about writing.

Then, a few months ago, as my list grew to 80, a friend said, "Have you thought about texting those little truisms out to a few friends?" Within a few days, I hired a firm that does this sort of thing. They set it all up. All I have to do is go in and type in these statements and program them to go out. Now hundreds of men and women receive one each day, at 3:00 Eastern time. If you'd like to receive them by text also, just let me know.

Then it became obvious that the best way to put all of these nuggets together in a helpful format would be to write a book. So here it is. I expanded the number to 100. I call them Recovery Rules. I don't expect you to read each one and say, "Oh my, this is brilliant! I never thought of that before!" But I am hopeful that you will find just a little bit of strength and hope each day as you reflect on a different Recovery Rule.

That's how I'd read this if I were you – one Rule per day.

I have written several other books on recovery, along with countless blogs and articles. But this has been my favorite project – hands down. My prayer is that as you walk your own road of recovery, these short nuggets will encourage you and give you hope to walk a little further, climb a little higher, and dig a little deeper.

Let's get after it. One hundred Recovery Rules.

RULE #1

If you are 90 percent in, you're 100 percent out.

"Give 100 percent. 110 percent is impossible. Only idiots recommend that."
Ron Swanson, Parks and Recreation, Season 3

While it's true that you can't give 110 percent to anything, you can get close. I don't think there is anything I say more than this – *if you are 90 percent in, you are 100 percent out.* In school, a 90 is pretty good. But in recovery, it's an 'F.' Let me illustrate.

Let's say you're a recovering sex addict. Your wife goes out of town for a week. When she returns, she wants to know if you were sober while she was gone. You are prepared for that question, and you've done the math.

"Honey, I've got great news. Out of the 168 hours that make up a week, I was faithful 99 percent of the time. I was only with another woman for about an hour and a half."

The reason people fail in recovery is that they treat sobriety like a hobby. We want to sprinkle in a little recovery work, so long as it doesn't demand too much from us.

Bill Murray is right: "The only time you should give less than 100 percent is when you are giving blood."

The secret to recovery is consistency. You have to go all in every day. You can't take a day off. That's why I start every day by saying recovery prayers and reading a devotional before my feet hit the ground. Consistency is everything. Coach John Wooden was speaking about basketball, but his advice works for recovery just as well. He told his players, "You have to give 100 percent every day. If you only give 75 percent today, you can't give 125 percent tomorrow to make up for it."

Though you and I may have never met, I know two things about you. I know you can find lasting sobriety, and I know it won't happen unless you give it 100 percent.

RULE #2

Without God, you can't. Without you, God won't.

"I can do all things through Christ, who gives me strength."
Philippians 4:13

St. Augustine said, "Work as though it all depends on you, and pray as though it all depends on God."

All recovery is spiritual. That is why seven of the twelve Steps refer to a Higher Power. Sadly, a record low of 81 percent of Americans believe in God (Gallop), but among addicts that number is much higher. In fact, according to the *Journal of Religion and Health*, 73% of addiction treatment programs in the U.S. include a spirituality-based element.

The role of faith in recovery cannot be overstated. Brian and Melissa Grim, of Baylor University, found that 84% of scientific studies cite faith as a positive factor in addiction prevention.

But if recovery was entirely up to God, we'd all be doing well. That's not how it works. God can heal us without our cooperation, but he won't. Have you noticed that the people God has given the most sobriety are also the ones who go to meetings and work a solid program of recovery?

Recovery is a partnership. You *can't* do it without God, and God *won't* do it without you.

What you need is balance. I suggest the following plan for lasting sobriety.

- Pray the 3rd Step Prayer every day.
- Pray the 7th Step Prayer every day.
- Pray the Serenity Prayer every day.
- Read recovery material every day.
- Make a call every day.
- Get to at least one meeting each week.

Pray and work. Work and pray. Do both. You can experience lasting sobriety and successful recovery. But you can't do it on your own, and God won't force it upon you. Work your program while you walk with God. You can do this. You can do all things through Christ who gives you strength.

RULE #3

Failure is a detour, not a dead end.

"Success is not final. Failure is not fatal. It is the courage to continue that counts."
Winston Churchill

When you relapse, it feels like your world has ended. "Back to square one," we say.

Not so fast.

Imagine you were running a marathon. If, on mile 21, you tripped and skinned your knee, what would you do next?

A. Go back to the starting line and begin the race all over again.
B. Brush yourself off and pick up where you fell.

I would do neither, because I would never make it to mile 21. But I digress.

No one does recovery perfectly. Stop me if you've heard this before: *it's about progress, not perfection.* Robert Kennedy had it right: "Only those who dare to fail greatly can ever achieve greatly."

Let's consider a couple of academic studies on the role of failure in recovery. A 2017 study published in the *Journal of Behavioral Decision Making* concluded that there is value in failure, but only if we sit with it for a while and learn from it. In other words, failure does not breed success, unless we find a lesson to build on in the future.

A 2016 review published in *Clinical Psychology Review* unpacked 46 separate studies on what works in overcoming failure. They concluded that a "more positive attributional style" helped to overcome failure. This means we discover what the failure can be attributed to, and move on.

You have had days of great success in battling your addiction. And you have had days that didn't go so well. It's how you view the bad days that matters most. You can see them as a dead end. The enemy would be thrilled if you viewed life that way. Or you can see every failure for what it is – a detour on your road to your ultimate goal. That goal has not changed. The route may have changed, but not your destination.

RULE #4

Your past performance is no guarantee of future results.

"You can never plan the future by the past."
Edmund Burke

We've all seen the ads on television. An investment group pushes their product with testimonies of how their gold, silver, Crypto, or investment strategy has produced a 500% return in the last two months. Then there is this tag line they are forced to say at the end.

"Past performance is no guarantee of future results."

In fact, a study published by *Forbes* found the opposite is often true. Many times, past performance completely flips in the future, based on the changing economic winds.

What is true in investments is true in sports. In 2001, the New England Patriots won the Super Bowl, after three-time Pro Bowler Drew Bledsoe was injured, and replaced by the 199th pick in the draft. Perhaps you've heard of him – Tom Brady.

After winning the Super Bowl, it was assumed the Patriots had begun a new dynasty. Not so fast. The next year, they didn't even make the playoffs.

Have you ever known someone who had years of sobriety, but then lost it? Sure you have. Perhaps that's you.

I'll never forget how proud I was to get my 8-month chip. "I'll never relapse," I said to myself. And then I did. Praise God, that was a long time ago, and there have been no slips or relapses since, but I know I am still vulnerable.

The answer is to keep doing what's working. I plan to attend 12-Step meetings for the rest of my life. Then, if they have them in heaven, I'll attend meetings there as well. Why? Because I know that past performance is no guarantee of future results.

RULE #5

Addiction isn't a bad problem; it's a bad solution.

"If I was having a bad day, eating was like self-medicating."
Al Roker

There's an old saying that when a man knocks on the door of a brothel, he is hoping to find God on the other side of the door.

Addiction is a problem. But mostly, it is a solution. A bad solution, but still a solution. We turn to our addiction to numb a pain, fill an emptiness, or mask a flaw. And then our solution *becomes* our problem.

History is full of examples of solutions that became problems. A certain red dye made M&Ms look more appealing. Then it was discovered that there was a link between this dye and cancer. Agent Orange started out as a good idea. It was a herbicide used by the military to cut through the forest so they could get a better view of the enemy. But the side effects still plague millions of veterans today. Asbestos found common use in construction projects until it was determined that it caused severe breathing problems. The substance was banned in 1989.

In each case, what started as a solution became the problem.

You didn't wake up one day and say, "I believe I'll become an addict." No, you were driven into your addiction by a myriad of factors. You may have fallen victim to parental neglect, physical abuse, or some other kind of trauma. Make no apologies for your addiction. But if you don't do something about it, that's on you.

Your addiction will take you further than you want to go, cost you more than you want to pay, and keep you longer than you want to stay. The price you will pay for living in your addiction brings compound interest. It only gets worse. Every day you act out will add more time to your sentence. It will take that much longer to break free.

I suggest you do two things. First, get professional help in determining what the real problems are. Second, find a better solution to your problems than an addiction that will cost you everything. I'm still waiting to meet the person who says, "In my pain I turned to addiction, and I'm sure glad I did!"

If another drink, pill, casino, cheeseburger, or porn image would really help, the last drink, pill, casino, cheeseburger, or porn image would have worked. But it didn't. Your solution has turned into a really bad problem.

RULE #6

You can blame someone else, but it won't help.

"People with a style of denial and blaming are definitely on the list of unsafe people to avoid."
Henry Cloud

You can blame all sorts of people for the trouble you've seen – the butcher, the baker, the candlestick maker. You can blame your mom, your dad, cousins, second cousins, aunts, uncles, and more. I have delved into my own family history and determined that much of our system of family secrecy goes back to the family cover-up of my grandfather's behaviors. I'd love to blame him for my addiction, and I'd probably tell him to his face, had he not died 12 years before I was born.

Here's the bottom line. You can blame someone else for your addiction, but it won't help.

Did you hear about the man dying in quicksand? Three men walked by, and each offered to help. The first man tossed a book to the guy in the quicksand. The title of the book was *How I Got into the Quicksand*. I'm sure it would have been a fascinating read, had the guy had time to go through it.

The second man tossed the guy a rope. The sinking man was appreciative, but the rope didn't help him very much since there was no one on the other end of that rope.

Finally, the third man came through for him. He tossed the man one end of his rope, while holding the other end. He then pulled the man to safety.

The man in the quicksand found safety by grabbing a rope, not by assigning blame to whoever pushed him into the sand, left him in the sand, or observed him in the sand.

Dr. Bernard Golden, expert on anger management, writes, "Blaming others distracts us from the constructive but difficult task of self-reflection."

John Gottman identified the four most destructive behaviors in relationships:

- Criticism
- Contempt
- Defensiveness
- Stonewalling

The theme of these four behaviors is blame. You can blame others for the pit you are in, but it really won't help.

RULE #7

What you think today, you'll do tomorrow.

*"Sow a thought and you reap an action; sow an act and you reap
a habit; sow a habit and you reap a character; sow a character
and you reap a destiny."*
Ralph Waldo Emerson

Addiction is more about what you think than what you do.
In my years of working with recovering addicts, one thing is constant. Every relapse is the predicable outcome of what the addict
was doing – and thinking – in the last few hours and days.
Addiction always follows the same cycle:

1. I think it.
2. I plan it.
3. I do it.
4. I hate it.
5. I cover it.
6. I do it again.

It all begins with a thought. *Forbes* contributor Nicole Serena
Silver writes, "A shift in your mindset can be profound for the outcomes you are wanting. Every experience begins with a thought."

The key is to turn your thoughts into a positive. Just as destructive thoughts fuel relapse, healthy thoughts fuel recovery. Whatever you feed will eventually grow.

Always the optimist, former first lady Eleanor Roosevelt said, "The future belongs to those who believe in the beauty of their dreams." And that's where it begins. If you just try to keep out all thoughts of alcohol, sex, food, or drugs, you'll go crazy. The way to avoid *destructive* thoughts is to replace them with *constructive* thoughts.

It's what we call thought replacement. You should always have a wholesome, positive thought ready to pull up, every time an intrusive thought tries to take up residence in your mind. The best way to secure a sober day tomorrow is to think sober thoughts today.

RULE #8

If you can stay sober for 20 minutes, you can make it.

"Any kind of novelty or excitement drives up dopamine in the brain."
Helen Fisher

When you feel the urge to act out, it seems like that temptation will last forever. The good news is that it doesn't. It's all about dopamine and the neural pathways of your brain.

Bill Nye explains, "You start doing the addictive behavior to feel good and then your receptors get overloaded with dopamine, then you stop doing the addictive thing and some of the receptors shut down and you don't have enough dopamine to feel good. So then you feel bad and go back to the addictive behavior to get more dopamine."

Translation – the dopamine rush doesn't last.

When you are triggered by a memory, something you see, or something you feel, remember this critical truth. The urge will pass. It always does, usually within 20 minutes. Here's the key – if you can stay sober for 20 minutes, you can make it.

I have created something I call the 20/20 rule. If you will do some of the following 20 things for 20 minutes, you can stay sober for those 20 minutes. And if you can stay sober for 20 minutes, you can stay sober for a lifetime.

Here are 20 things you can try to stay sober for 20 minutes:

- Go for a walk.
- Make a call.
- Pray the 3rd Step Prayer.
- Read from the Life Recovery Bible.
- Journal.Sing a praise song to the Lord.
- Text five people you know from recovery.
- Pray the Serenity Prayer.
- Read through Step 4 in a 12-Step book.
- Think through the end game of acting out.
- Go for a short drive.
- Update your middle circle.
- Watch "Flawless" by MercyMe.
- Do a short exercise.
- Pray for five people in recovery.
- Fix a snack.
- Pray the 7th Step Prayer.
- Write three reasons to not act out.
- Read a chapter from this book.
- Listen to a recovery podcast.

RULE #9

The opposite of addiction is connection.

"Even the Lone Ranger didn't do it alone."

Harvey MacKay

From 1949 to 1957, it was one of the most popular shows in the early days of television. *The Lone Ranger* featured a masked former Texas Ranger who fought outlaws in the Old West. The show debuted on a Detroit radio station in 1933, before eventually migrating to television. The main character was played by Clayton Moore (for all but one season). But as great as he was, the Lone Ranger didn't do it by himself. He relied heavily on his sidekick, Tonto, as well as Silver, his iconic horse.

Recovery is a team sport. My friend, Michael Leahy, is the founder of Bravehearts. In a study he commissioned, it was found that one in 10,000 find sobriety without the help of another person. And I would argue that even if you could *find* sobriety on your own, you can't *keep* sobriety on your own.

Tristan Hayes, author for Integrated Addiction Care, said, "When the addict finds that they are not alone and no longer have to fight their dependence on their own, their lives become open to a world of possibilities."

That you were created for connection should not come as a surprise. The God who said, "It is not good that man should be alone" (Genesis 2:18) has provided all kinds of ways to find connection: support groups, church, work, community projects, service organizations, hobby clubs, and more.

Gregory Walton, of Stanford University, did an interesting study, in which he found that when college students believed they shared a birthday with another student, they were more motivated to complete a task with that student and performed better on the task. The same was true for children age four and five.

What do we learn from this study? We learn what we already knew. We are wired for connection. The next time you are tempted to indulge in your addiction of choice, don't think "sobriety." Think "connection." Make a call. Attend a meeting. Find a group. Go to church. Get outside of yourself. Find that human connection that your soul so desperately needs. You can win this battle, but you can't do it by yourself.

RULE #10

God allows what he hates in order to accomplish what he loves.

"As for you, you meant evil against me, but God meant it for good, to bring it about that many people should be kept alive, as they are today."
Genesis 50:20

When you hurt, God hurts. When you hit rock bottom, were discovered in your addiction, or were arrested, the heart of God broke for your pain. But he allowed it to happen for your greater good. God allows what he hates in order to accomplish what he loves. If you had not hit bottom, you would have never found recovery. Call that a win.

An unknown author gave us this compelling poem many years ago. It still speaks to us today. It is titled *When God Wants to Drill a Man*.

When God wants to drill a man,
And thrill a man,
And skill a man.
When God wants to mold a man
To play the noblest part.

When he yearns with all his heart
To create so great and bold a man
That all the world shall be amazed,
Watch his methods, watch his ways!

How he ruthlessly perfects
Whom he royally elects!
How he hammers him and hurts him,
And with mighty blows converts him.

Into trial shapes of clay which
Only God understands;
While his tortured heart is crying,
And he lifts beseeching hands!

How he bends but never breaks
When his good he undertakes;
How he uses whom he chooses,
And which every purpose fuses him;
By every act induces him
To try his splendor out.
God knows what he's about.

Don't miss that last line. *"God knows what he's about."* We see only a piece of the puzzle, while God sees the finished product. Trust the process when it's easy and when it's hard. Trust God when you see him and when you don't. Never forget that while God hates the pain of the process, he loves the finished product.

RULE #11

Don't commit to a lifetime; commit to a day.

*"I have a new philosophy. I'm only going to dread
one day at a time."*
Charlie Brown

I was in a 12-Step meeting several years ago, when a man gave his sobriety date during the check-in time. But rather than give a date or measure his sobriety in years, he said, "Today, I have been sober for 1,368 days."

I like that. Sobriety is a one-day-at-a-time proposition. I have often told my wife, "I'm not saying I'll never act out again, I'm just saying it won't be today."

We find similar advice from men whose successes have been diverse and monumental. From President Abe Lincoln: "The best thing about the future is that it comes one day at a time." And from tennis great Rafael Nadal: "My motivation is tomorrow, just one day at a time."

Taking recovery one day at a time means waking up and re-committing to the process every single day. This means that despite whatever stressful circumstances you may be facing in life, and regardless of what happened yesterday, you are making the conscious choice to carry on in your commitment to sobriety. It is a choice you make again every morning.

Make this your prayer today:

- I will seek God today.
- I will avoid my middle circle today.
- I will practice good self-care today.
- I will pray the Serenity Prayer today.
- I will do something kind today, for someone who cannot repay me.

It's not enough to commit to sobriety for today. You need to be specific. What will you do, exactly, to build your recovery for the next 24 hours?

RULE #12

Bounce your eyes.

"What we see depends mainly on what we look for."
John Lubbock

You don't have to be a sex addict in order to struggle with your eyes. Steven Arterburn wrote a great book several years ago, titled *Every Man's Battle*. Not *The Sex Addict's Battle*, but *Every Man's Battle*. We all struggle to maintain custody of our eyes. Arterburn explains, "The problem is that your eyes have always bounced toward the sexual, and you've made no attempt to end this habit. To combat it, you need to build a reflex action by training your eyes to immediately bounce away from the sexual, like the jerk of your hand away from a hot stove."

Job made a commitment with his eyes. "I have made a covenant with my eyes that I would not sin against God by looking lustfully at a young woman" (Job 31:1). William Shakespeare said it like this: "The eyes are the window to your soul."

I have come up with a specific formula. I call it the "3-second rule." Here's how it works. When you are triggered by something visual, immediately count to three. Make sure your eyes are somewhere else by the time you get to three.

You can do this. No one has control over your eyes except you. Every time you stare in the wrong direction, that is a choice you don't have to make. Learn to focus on sights that are pure and healthy. If you don't, you will be creating a new file of images that your brain, your largest sex organ, will go back to in weak moments. The best way to overcome tempting visuals is to not create new ones. Eventually, you will reprogram your mind, and bouncing your eyes will become natural.

Pray for God's strength. Stay diligent. Be on alert. Know your surroundings. I don't know anyone who has complete control of his eyes every single time. It's another progress, not perfection thing. But you can do it. Go ahead. Make a covenant with your eyes.

RULE #13

You won't come to the beginning of your recovery until you come to the end of yourself.

"When we come to the end of self
we come to the beginning of Christ."
Charles Spurgeon

Jesus asked the paralytic, "Do you want to get well?" (John 5:6). Notice, Jesus didn't ask him if he wanted to *be* well, but if he was ready to *get* well. We all want to be well – no more drugs, gambling, overeating, self-harm, affairs, etc. But it's the process of getting well that transforms hope into reality.

I have yet to meet the addict who found successful recovery until he hit bottom. J.K. Rowling, the creator of Harry Potter, said, "Rock bottom became the solid foundation on which I rebuilt my life."

I consider my addiction to be God's great unwanted gift. I didn't ask for it. My addiction was the predictable result of my trauma, isolation, and abuse. No one signs up for that. But this has been the one challenge I've had in life that I absolutely could not overcome apart from going all in with surrender. I had to come to the end of myself before I could come to the beginning of my recovery.

Thomas Koulopoulos, founder of Delphi Group, writes, "None of us ask for life's greatest challenges, but that doesn't mean we can't benefit from them."

You have faced many challenges in life; we all have. But this thing called "addiction" is your biggest foe. It is powerful, cunning, and relentless. Addiction never takes a day off. And the day you think you have it whipped is the day you just lost the battle. Addiction is progressive; so is recovery. You can collect chips, but you don't get to check a box. The road of recovery continues on, and that's a good thing. That's what keeps us humble and alert.

If you have crashed and burned, thank God for that. If something inside you has died, rejoice. We serve a God who masters in resurrections.

RULE #14

Focus on what can be, not on what has been.

"The future is not something we enter.
The future is something we create."
Leonard Sweet

When I was a kid, I rode my bicycle everywhere. That was an era when it was considered safe to do so. I loved to ride up hills, across fields, and across town. But the one thing I could never do was sit still. Try to stop on a bike, without putting your foot down, and you'll fall over.

Albert Einstein said, "Life is like riding a bicycle. To keep your balance, you must keep moving."

Recovery is the same way. You can't move forward by sitting still. Or by looking back. It's true that you need to learn from your past. But don't live there.

C.S. Lewis was right: "There are far, far better things ahead than any we leave behind."

But you can't just wait on your future to happen. Your future is something that must be created. There are several ways you can do that.

1. Read a new book.
2. Join a new group.
3. Plan a Recovery Day.

4. Find a new hobby.
5. Join a service organization.
6. Volunteer to serve at your church.
7. Start a journal.

The fact that you're still here proves God has big plans for you. He is more committed to your future than you are. But you need to be proactive. Your future – marked by years of sobriety and recovery – won't just happen. You have to create it by making wise choices. It is only by doing things you've never done that you'll go places you've never been.

RULE #15

You make your choices, then your choices make you.

"Your life changes the moment you make a new, congruent, and committed decision."
Tony Robbins

Too many of us are captive to our conditions. But there is one thing that trumps conditions every time.

Decisions.

Stephen Covey writes, "We are the creative force of our lives, and through our own decisions rather than our conditions, if we carefully learn to do certain things, we can accomplish those goals."

We have all suffered through difficult conditions, not of our choosing. I didn't choose to lose my dad when I was still a teenager. I didn't choose to be abused sexually by a neighborhood boy when I was eight or nine. I didn't ask to be legally blind in junior high school, or to have a speech impediment until I was 15. These were not choices; they were conditions.

For too long, I remained captive to these conditions. It took decades for me to understand that my conditions do not rule me. Only my decisions can do that. Life is 10 percent what happens to us, and 90 percent how we respond.

In order to make the right decisions, you need to start with the right questions. I suggest the two greatest questions you can ever ask.

1. What is the wise thing to do?
2. What do you think is the wise thing to do?

You usually know the wise thing to do. Addicts rarely fail because we don't know what to do. We fail because we don't do what we know. But when in doubt, pause and ask yourself that question: "What is the wise thing to do?"

Sometimes (rarely) you won't know the answer to that question. When this happens, go find someone you know and trust. Then try the second greatest question. Ask them, "What do you think is the wise thing to do?"

Through wisdom, you discover the right choices to make in life. Make those choices, then those choices will make you.

RULE #16

Until you take ownership for your disease, you won't take responsibility for your recovery.

"Dear Math, grow up and solve your own problems."
Anonymous

Brett and Kate McKay wrote a compelling article, "Personal Responsibility 102: The Importance of Owning Up to Your Mistakes and How to Do It." They write, "You can't learn from your mistakes if you can't acknowledge you've made them. And if you don't learn from your mistakes, you're destined to repeat them. That's a recipe for quickly going nowhere in life."

"I own it."

Those may be the three hardest words for any of us to say. We can blame others for the things that led to our addictions, but that won't help. It may be true, but it won't help. At some point, we all have to say those three all-powerful words.

"I own it."

I don't know anyone who jumped into addiction willfully. But I also don't know anyone who got out the moment they knew what was happening. One study found that the average addict lives in his addiction for 18 years before seeking help. During those 18 years, he blames others, makes excuses, and dabbles in recovery. But he can't bring himself to say those three transformative words.

"I own it."

If you are still treating recovery as a hobby, that can all change today. This can be the start of a lifelong journey marked by victory and overcoming. But for that to happen, you have to quit making excuses. No more blame game. No more minimizing. No more avoidance. You must look beyond the past, the pain, and the problems. In order to embrace a better future, say these three simple words.

"I own it."

RULE #17

God won't use you despite your past, but because of it.

"The only way to get rid of your past is to make a future out of it. God will waste nothing."
Phillips Brooks

I work with a lot of pastors in recovery. Not long ago, a pastor described his addictive behaviors to me, followed by this question: "Do you think what I've done disqualifies me from ministry?"

I answered, "You were never qualified in the first place."

I lost my pastoral ministry of 31 years because of my addiction. The pain of that moment stays with me. But I use it as a positive. I never want to feel that pain again. But in the years that have followed, something shocking has taken place. I have gone through three phases.

1. God can't use me because of my past.
2. God can use me despite my past.
3. God will use me because of my past.

In late 2014, my pastoral ministry ended. But my ministry did not end. It was just getting started. Today, I get to write a daily recovery devotional that is read in 25 countries. I get to work with

130 men in recovery – every week. That is double the size of the average church in America. Beth and I get to work with couples in recovery. And I have met more authentic men these past few years, doing recovery work, than I ever did before.

The Bible is full of men and women whom God used, not *despite* their past, but *because* of it. One of those men was a guy who made a career out of persecuting Christians. Then everything changed, and he became the most significant figure in early Christianity. His name was Paul, and he summarized his transformation with these words: "Forgetting what is behind and reaching forward to what is ahead, I pursue as my goal the prize promised by God's heavenly call in Christ Jesus" (Philippians 3:13-14).

Embrace your story. What God allowed, he will redeem. There is someone who needs to hear your story, because it is full of hope. Don't keep it to yourself. Find ways to be used to help others. After all, an addiction is a terrible thing to waste. It once made you *bitter*. Now you are *better*. And God will use you in ways he never could have before.

RULE #18

Isolation is not a condition; it's a choice.

"Anyone in recovery knows that isolation is the biggest enemy."
Ivan Moody

Dr. Gary Wenk, contributor for *Psychology Today*, reports on an interesting study on the socialization needs of monkeys. He writes, "Monkeys raised in partial or total isolation since birth were hostile toward others and could not form adequate social attachments in adolescence or adulthood. The degree of social damage was related to the duration of social isolation. Sophisticated neuroimaging analyses of humans and monkeys revealed structural alterations in two critical brain regions for normal social interactions and emotional control, the prefrontal cortex and amygdala."

To summarize Dr. Wenk's findings, when we fail to experience healthy connections with others, this leaves a wound that can take decades to heal.

You were created for socialization. While a number of factors may have driven you into isolation, none of them can keep you there. Only you can do that. Isolation is not a condition; it is a choice. Isolation is the result of a series of bad choices.

Here are a few good choices you can make to improve your connection with others.

1. Join a 12-Step group.
2. Serve in that 12-Step group.
3. Arrive early to your 12-Step meeting.
4. Stay late at your next 12-Step meeting.

Do you see a trend here? Join a 12-Step group. Or check out one of my Freedom Groups. But don't just show up. Get involved. Find a sponsor. Become a sponsor. Exchange phone numbers with others in the group. Get outside yourself. Make a connection. Isolation is not your friend. Nor is it a condition. It is a choice. But isolation is a choice you don't have to make.

RULE #19

Free cheese is always available in the mousetrap.

"The early bird gets the worm,
but the second mouse gets the cheese."
Willie Nelson

Don't fall for it. It's a trick. Call it "bait and switch." The cheese looks good, smells good, and tastes good. And it's free. But it's not worth it. It's a trap – a mousetrap. And I have yet to meet a mouse who said, "That whole mousetrap thing was worth it for the brief moment when I enjoyed the cheese."

Addiction comes at a price. A heavy price. The National Institute on Drug Abuse estimates that addiction costs America about $600 billion every year. And the Substance Abuse and Mental Health Services says that drug abuse alone costs us $151 billion each year.

Mousetraps come in three shapes.

1. People: There are certain people who are a trap for you. They are tempting, but also toxic. They can be found everywhere, even at church. These are people who will bring you down. They may say all the right things, but at the end of the day, they are to be avoided at all costs.

2. Places: There are certain places you need to avoid. If you are addicted to alcohol, stay out of the bar. If food is your problem, don't shop alone. If gambling has become an addiction, find concerts somewhere other than at a casino. If you are a sex addict, the beach is probably not the best place to hang out.

3. Predicaments: You know some circumstances in which you are most vulnerable. There are predicaments that need to be avoided. Some of these may include: time alone with the opposite sex, social media, certain movie channels, parties with alcohol, certain groups of people, and carrying extra cash.

Yes, there's always free cheese in the mousetrap. The key is to recognize the mousetrap when you see it. Better yet, know where the mousetraps are, and stay clear of those people, places, and predicaments. The cheese is free, but costly. It's not worth it. It never was.

RULE #20

If you live for the approval of others, you will die from their rejection.

"You wouldn't worry so much about what others think of you if you realized how seldom they do."
Eleanor Roosevelt

I admit it. I'm a card-carrying people-pleaser. And I'm really good at it. That comes with years of practice and experience. I did it as a pastor. My last church had over 2,000 members. And every year, every one of them got a hand-written birthday card from me. I visited every hospital, even though we had a man on staff for that. I went to every Student Camp, even though we had a Student Pastor for that. I attended every Christmas party, every concert, every children's event.

And don't get me started on community involvement. I was a Rotarian, but I also attended meetings for the Lion's Club and Kiwanis. During one of my pastorates, my community was hit by a horrific storm, so the mayor appointed me the head of the community recovery committee. I served on the Boards for the Boy's Club, MLK Day, and two universities. I was glad to sit on countless denominational committees. Add numerous random assignments on my alma mater's Alumni Board, community projects, and Little League coaching, and that all adds up to a really good people-pleaser, totally incapable of saying "No."

Why does this matter? Among other things, this set me up for stress, which demanded self-medication. People-pleasers make really good addicts.

Are you a people-pleaser? If any of the following describes you, you probably are.

- Lack of self-care
- Hard to make decisions due to self-doubt
- Tolerate toxic relationships
- Struggle with sharing feelings honestly
- Fear of rejection that can be crippling

To beat addiction, you need to untangle yourself from the shackles of people-pleasing. Practice self-care. Learn to say "No." Love others *as you love yourself*, not *before you love yourself*. Do the things that keep you healthy, in mind, body, and spirit. Never forget, if you aren't good to yourself, you won't have anything to give anyone else.

RULE #21

Yesterday's chains do not bind you; only today's choices can do that.

*"Chains of habit are too light to be felt
until they are too heavy to be broken."*
Warren Buffett

The Bible records a crazy encounter Jesus had with a man in a cemetery. He ran around naked and was a threat to everyone who came near. They tried to chain him, but the chains did not work. "He had often been bound with shackles and chains, and the chains had been torn apart by him and the shackles broken in pieces, and no one was strong enough to subdue him" (Mark 5:4).

Anyone who has lived a life of addiction can understand the metaphor of being bound by chains. But there is good news. Jennifer Rothschild said it well: "God's love is bigger than our failures and stronger than any chains that bind us."

The question becomes, what do we have to do to break free from the chains of addiction? Psychologist Dr. Rodney Luster produced a helpful work titled, "Breaking the Chains of Addiction." He suggests, "Ultimately, breaking the chain of addiction and compulsion requires our full conviction, and we have to want to be free of it before we ever start trying."

Did you catch that? The key to breaking free is desire. We must want to be free. But it goes further than that. It is the decisions we make as a result of our desire that put points on the board. Choices cut both ways. They can bring freedom or they can keep us in chains.

The good news is that freedom is a choice. You are just as sober as you really want to be. If you want sobriety badly enough, you will have it. You will do the next right thing. You will take the steps that are necessary to live a life of recovery.

Don't play the part of a victim. You are a victor in Christ. Recovery won't be easy, but it will be possible. Whether you make it or not is up to you. It is the decisions of the future that matter now, not the chains of the past.

RULE #22

Relapse is not an event, but a process.

*"You can't go back and make a brand-new start,
but you do get to make a brand-new ending."*
Carl Bard

Steven Adler said, "Part of recovery is relapse. I dust myself off and move forward again."

I'm not sure I agree with Adler's implication. While everyone I know has experienced some form of relapse since their initial commitment to sobriety, relapse is not inevitable. You don't ever have to slip or relapse again.

It is important to understand the process of relapse, in order to avoid it altogether. And that's the key word – *process*. Relapse is a process, not an event. It doesn't just happen. Relapse is the outcome of a series of bad choices and lazy recovery work.

Samuel L. Jackson bravely told his story. He said, "I understood, through rehab, things about creating characters. I understood that creating whole people means knowing where we come from, how we can make a mistake, and how we overcome things to make ourselves stronger."

Part of Jackson's story is "knowing where we come from." It is that deep dive into our past and reflective consideration of where we are going that sets us up for a win.

Let's break it down. If relapse is a process, what does that process look like, exactly? It comes in three phases.

1. Emotional relapse: We are triggered on an emotional level. We feel lonely, isolated, angry, or threatened on some level. When we are emotionally dysregulated, we are the most vulnerable.
2. Mental relapse: Remember the cycle of relapse we talked about earlier? We think it, plan it, do it, hate it, cover it, then do it again. It starts in the mind. What we think today, we do tomorrow.
3. Physical relapse: What we feel and think leads to what we do – the next drink, pill, or porn image. But it is critical that we understand relapse never starts here. Physical relapse is the inevitable result of emotional and mental relapse.

RULE #23

God loves you more than he hates your mess.

"You don't have the ability to make God not love you."
Matt McMillen

I'm not going to soften the truth. God hates your mess. He hates what it has done to you, your family, and your reputation. He hates the carnage, trauma, and pain. He hates every wound, every scar, and every memory that torments you and those closest to you. He hates it all.

But more than he hates your mess, he loves you. You couldn't make God not love you if you tried. Paul wrote, "Nothing can separate us from the love of God which is in Christ Jesus" (Romans 8:29). Nothing. Nada. Zero. Zilch. Nothing.

But in the addict's mind, none of this makes sense. Matt McMillen writes, "We can't understand God's love in our finite minds, especially when we keep messing up. We think that he will leave us or he won't love us anymore."

That's why we must return to Scripture. In our shame, we think we don't deserve God's love. And that's true. We don't. But we have it anyway.

Let me share one of the most profound thoughts I've ever had. *Nothing I can ever do will make God love me more, and nothing I have ever done has made him love me less.*

Why does this matter? It matters because it leads us to one conclusion. God's grace will take us as we are, but his love won't leave us that way. Ultimately, love beats mess. So bring your mess to God. Then leave it there. Don't drop your mess off with sticky hands. Let it go. Walk away from it all, into a whole new way of life.

Let's review. Repeat these statements. Make them your own.

- I don't have the ability to make God not love me.
- Nothing I can ever do will make him love me less.
- God loves me more than he hates my mess.

RULE #24

Lust writes checks it cannot cash.

"Lust enters as a house guest,
then becomes a host,
and then a master."
Khalil Gibran

Sexaholics Anonymous defines sobriety as "progressive victory over lust." I like that. The point is not really that we not act out with our bodies, but that we don't act out with our minds. Lust fails to satisfy – every time. It's like drinking salt water, hoping to quench our thirst.

But most of us are slow learners. President Jimmy Carter said what most of us were thinking. "I've looked on many women with lust. I've committed adultery in my heart many times. God knows I will do this and forgives me."

The good news is that lust is not inevitable. We know that "all that is in the world, the lust of the flesh, and the lust of the eyes, and the pride of life, is not from the Father" (1 John 2:16). Since lust is a violation of God's plan, we must have a choice. To lust or not to lust – that is the question.

What is the answer?

I've learned the hard way what the answer is *not*.

- It's not will power.
- It's not mind over matter.
- It's not self-discipline.

So what is it? Paul provides the answer. "Walk in the Spirit, and you shall not fulfill the lust of the flesh. For the flesh lusts against the Spirit, and the Spirit against the flesh; and these are contrary to each other" (Galatians 5:16-17).

In other words, what you feed will grow. Feed your lust and it will only get worst. By trying to get it out of your system, you will only get it into your system. So feed the right "beast."

Have you heard the story about the man with two dogs? They were identical, other than their colors. One was black and the other white. Each day, the owner had them race. Over time, each dog won exactly half the time. The man took bets from his neighbors on which dog would win each day. He would bet his own money, as well. And each day, whichever dog the owner bet on, won. Eventually, a neighbor asked, "How is it that you always know which dog is going to win the race?" The man explained, "It's whichever dog I feed last."

The same is true with you. Feed your lust and it will grow. Feed your soul and you will be victorious.

RULE #25

God cannot be found in the noise.

*"Noise proves nothing. Often a hen who has merely
laid an egg cackles as if she laid an asteroid."*
Mark Twain

Noise is not your friend. On the other hand, solitude is. Mother Teresa said, "We need to find God, and he cannot be found in noise and restlessness. God is the friend of silence. See how nature – trees, flowers, grass – grows in silence; see the stars, the moon and the sun, how they move in silence. We need silence to be able to touch souls."

Jack Fong, a sociologist at California State Polytechnic University, has studied solitude. His conclusions are interesting. "When people take these moments to explore their solitude, not only will they be forced to confront who they are, they just might learn a little bit about how to out-maneuver some of the toxicity that surrounds them in a social setting."

Let's get specific. How, exactly, do we "out-maneuver our toxicity"?

The simple answer is found in one of the most memorable psalms. "Be still and know that I am God" (Psalm 46:10).

Let's take that a little further. I have found that solitude must be scheduled. It doesn't just happen. I have to schedule quiet moments when I can sit in God's presence, shutting out all the noise. I must do this:

- Daily – time in the Word and prayer
- Weekly – church worship service
- Monthly – recovery day
- Yearly – annual retreat

Now it's your turn. What will you do to shut out the noise, this day, this week, this month, and this year? I suggest a written, specific plan. Again, solitude doesn't just happen. You have to make it happen. This would be a good time to start.

RULE #26

Addiction cripples, but secrets kill.

"Secrets have the power to kill, the power to destroy.
We each hold nuclear weapons inside of us."
J.M. Darhower

Nothing will destroy a marriage like secrets. As I often say, an ugly truth beats a pretty lie every time. Dr. Chandni Tugnait, a psychotherapist and life coach, offers several effects that secrets have on personal relationships.

1. Loss of trust
2. Resentment
3. Unmet needs
4. Lack of communication
5. Emotional distance

If I could have included a magic wand in this book, I would have. I wish you could wave a wand and suddenly become more honest, more transparent, more authentic. But secrets are the common denominator of every addiction. We think, "I'd rather be loved than known." But the fact is, you can't be authentically loved *until* you are known.

There are many ways in which you can do this. Start by being honest with yourself. Come clean every day. Admit your weaknesses, sins, and flaws. Then be honest with God. He probably knows your secrets anyway! Every day, confess your sins to him. Hold nothing back.

But you also need to come clean with another human being. Call him or her an accountability partner. Give this person permission to ask you the hard questions. "Have you had a slip today?" "Did you get on an inappropriate website today?" "Are you hiding anything from your spouse?"

Then there's one more step. You need a group. When Jesus healed the paralytic, he did it in a crowd. When he raised Jairus' daughter, he did it in front of witnesses. Jesus understood the power of connection. You need a group. Call it a recovery group, a 12-Step group, or a support group. Whatever you call it, you need a group.

I am often asked, "Which is the best group to join?" I answer, "The one you will attend." The connection and accountability that come with a group is the perfect antidote for keeping secrets.

RULE #27

Your current strategy is perfectly suited for the results you are getting.

"Everyone has a plan until they get punched in the mouth."
Mike Tyson

Successful recovery is not a mystery. Neither is relapse. Your sobriety or failure is the product of your strategy. I can't say that enough. The name of our ministry is There's Still Hope. I love that name. And it's true. No matter what you've done or how far you've fallen, there's still hope. If you have hit bottom, fallen off the wagon, or blown up your marriage, there's still hope.

But Vince Lombardi was right: "Hope is not a strategy."

If you are not satisfied with your recovery, do something about it. Change your strategy. Join a new group. Listen to a new podcast. Do some additional reading. Find a new therapist. Connect with another addict. Get a sponsor. Execute a better time with God each day.

Michael Porter explains, "Strategy is about making choices, trade-offs; it's about deliberately choosing to be different." Underline that word, "deliberately." Develop a strategy you will stick to.

Jim Rohn said, "Success is 20 percent skills and 80 percent strategy. You might know how to succeed, but more importantly, what's your plan?"

You might try ordering your strategy around a good set of S.M.A.R.T. goals. I'll spell it out for you. Good goals must be:

- Specific
- Measurable
- Achievable
- Relevant
- Time-based

Take a few minutes and devise a plan today, one which includes S.M.A.R.T. goals. Then formulate a strategy that will meet those goals. Put your strategy on paper. Get input from others. But more importantly, do what you say you will do. Follow the old leadership axiom – plan your work, then work your plan.

RULE #28

No matter how far you travel the road of recovery, the ditch is still just as close on either side of the road.

"Sometimes you fall into a ditch
without even knowing it's there."
Mohanlal

I've seen it happen too many times. So have you. A man or woman with long-term sobriety relapses. After several years of walking down the middle of Recovery Blvd, they fall into the ditch. It's true – no matter how far you go down the road to recovery, the ditch is still right there. It never goes anywhere.

There are a couple of ways to stay out of the ditch. First, stay within your guardrails. They are there for a reason. When we drive up a mountain road, the goal is to stay as far back from the guardrails as possible. The same works for recovery. Every now and then, you would be wise to revisit your guardrails. Fortify them as needed. Do what King Hezekiah did in 2 Chronicles. Build a second wall of defense.

You also need to pay attention to warning signs. They serve a purpose. When the sign reads, "Slow down," add caution to your recovery. When you see a sign that reads, "Sharp turn ahead," prepare for what's coming. Do whatever you have to do to stay in the middle of the road.

It helps us to stay out of the ditch if we know what that ditch looks like. Let's consider a few of the most common ditches for those in recovery.

- Distraction
- Denial
- Dependency
- Discouragement
- Disconnection

Never take your eye off the road. And never take your sobriety for granted. What has happened to others can happen to you. None of us is bullet-proof. Take heed, lest you fall. Stay in the middle of the road, never swerving toward the ditch on either side.

RULE #29

The journey of 1,000 miles begins with a single step.

"The secret to getting ahead is getting started."
Mark Twain

I'm a walker. I average five miles per day. I never miss 10,000 steps, apart from illness. As of this writing, I have not missed my goal of 10,000 daily steps for the last seven months. That sounds hard, perhaps. But it's really not. I never set out to walk 10,000 steps. What I do is to take the *next* step. The journey of 1,000 miles begins with a single step.

I love the way Tim Herrera says it. The scholarly author suggests, "Break down the very first steps you have to take and keep slicing them up into tiny, easily achievable micro-goals, then celebrate each achievement."

I love that word – micro-goals.

There are several ways to start your journey of recovery; there are several examples of micro-goals. For some, the first step is a session with a therapist who is well-trained in addiction recovery. For others, the first step is to get to a support group. Or it might be a call to someone who offers a recovery program. Whatever the first step looks like to you, take it!

Each day, you get to take a new first step. That might include praying the Serenity Prayer. Or working one of the 12 Steps. Or making a call. Usually, the first step isn't a big step. It's just a simple step in the right direction.

Take a few minutes to come up with your next micro-goal. What does it look like? How will you pursue this goal? What specific step will you take in the right direction? How will you trust God to keep you on track?

Now you need to set the time when you will take this step. Write down three things:

1. Your first step
2. When you'll do this
3. Where you'll do this

Recovery is not hard, if you break it down to micro-goals. Take one step today. Then another one tomorrow. Before you know it, you'll achieve a sobriety you never thought was possible.

RULE #30

You're only as healthy as your secrets.

"Man is not what he thinks he is, he is what he hides."
Andre Malraux

Can I be sober and still keep secrets? The long answer is, "No!"

I have taken four polygraphs as part of clinical disclosures early in my recovery. Those remain the greatest gifts I've ever given Beth. As my wife, she didn't need to know everything. She needed to *know* that she knew everything.

For each polygraph, I was asked an interesting question. "Since your last polygraph, have you lied to your group or your sponsor?" My therapist has the wisdom to know that any dishonesty paves the road for relapse. There are no small lies, and there are no insignificant secrets. Every secret counts.

Do our secrets hurt those closest to us? Sure, they do. But the first victim of every kept secret is the one who is harboring that secret. When you keep secrets from your spouse, you are hurting yourself more than you are hurting your spouse. That's because your secrets compromise your integrity, honesty, and authenticity. Your spouse is not really married to you, but to the cardboard cut-out.

That secrets render us fake, hypocritical, and inauthentic is not lost on leaders in the field.

Ruben Castaneda writes, "The harm is not connected specifically to the nature of the secret, but rather that people tend to think about whatever it is they're keeping hush-hush, which leads them to feel inauthentic."

Michael Stepian, assistant professor at Columbia Business School, conducted a study of 2,000 participants who kept a combined 13,000 secrets. His research concluded that when people mask who they are or what they've done, they have feelings of inauthenticity that harm relationships.

What secrets are you keeping? You need to get them out in order to be healthy. Start with your therapist. Then a trusted friend. Eventually, your spouse.

RULE #31

You need a Recovery Day each month.

"Life isn't about finding yourself. Life is about creating yourself."
George Bernard Shaw

I have a great sponsor. He led me through the 12 Steps several years ago, and though we now live 2,000 miles apart, he remains a consistent voice of wisdom and encouragement. In my early years of sobriety, he led me to do two things that have had enduring marks on my recovery. The first things he said I should do is to pray the 3rd Step Prayer, 7th Step Prayer, and Serenity Prayer every day. Each day, before my feet hit the floor, I pray all three prayers. And I repeat that exercise two more times each day.

But my sponsor's other recommendation has been even more transformational. "Have a Recovery Day each month," he said.

I said, "Great! What's a Recovery Day?"

He explained that a Recovery Day is a full day set apart to focus on recovery and self-care. While I don't do one every month, I do several each year. For me, the day always includes some recovery reading, meditation, and contemplation. I mix in other things like a nice drive, visiting a museum, or going to a ballgame. Often, I end the day with a long walk on the beach after sunset.

In my 90-Day Recovery Program, I tell clients to take a Recovery Day three times in the workbook. I believe in it that much.

Why? Because this is a concentrated time to be with God, shut out the cares of the world, and focus on personal growth.

Johann Wolfgang von Goethe said, "Everybody wants to be somebody, but nobody wants to grow."

My Recovery Day is one of the best opportunities to grow. What about you? What are you willing to do in order to grow? I suggest you stop now and plan a day within the next couple of weeks, when you can do your Recovery Day. Determine when you will do this, and what it will involve. Make your activities count. It's not enough to just take a day off from work. Use your time wisely. Do something on your Recovery Day that the following month will thank you for.

RULE #32

What you feed, grows; what you starve, dies.

"Change is inevitable. Growth is optional."
John Maxwell

Michael Leahy, founder of BraveHearts, has been an encourager and supporter of our ministry from Day 1. He has trained dozens of men and women through his patented mentoring program. I must credit Michael for Rule #32. I'm sure you have found this to be true in your life, your recovery, your marriage, your fitness program, your investment strategies and more.

What you feed will grow; what you starve will die.

How does this play out? The person who finds lasting recovery is not the brightest or strongest, but the hungriest.

When you feed your recovery with instructive podcasts, helpful therapy, and 12-Step work, you will find yourself growing in your sobriety. And when you starve yourself from all porn use, drug use, alcohol use, and anything else that drags you down, you experience an amazing freedom you otherwise never knew.

Yogi Berra said, "If all you do is what you've done, then all you'll get is what you've got."

The key to growth is a willingness to change. Charles Darwin observed, "It is not the strongest of the species that survive, nor the most intelligent, but the one most responsible to change."

Too many of us are more comfortable with the problem we know, rather than the solution we don't know. So we keep returning to the same old things and the same old people while making the same old mistakes.

Award-winning Wharton professor Katy Milkman says, "Change comes most readily when you understand what's standing between you and success and tailor your solution to that roadblock."

If you want to experience great freedom tomorrow, feed on this today:

- Recovery meetings
- Recovery readings
- Recovery podcasts
- Recovery coaching
- Recovery work

RULE #33

Sobriety is about what you stop. Recovery is about what you start.

"The goal is not to be sober. The goal is to love yourself enough that you don't need to drink."
Anonymous

"I'm white-knuckling it!"

That is the first thing I remember hearing from my early recovery meetings. It didn't take long to figure out what they were saying. And we've all been there. We have stayed sober (technically) by barely holding on. We just got through it, with no room to spare. We felt the heat, but didn't get burned. Whew! Close call!

While it is better to white-knuckle it than give in, God has a better plan. Don't just focus on what you're trying to stop. Focus on what you need to start.

That's the difference between sobriety and recovery. Sobriety is all about stopping unwanted behaviors. Recovery is about what you start. Sobriety means no more drugs, shopping, ice cream, or pornography. Pick your poison. Then refuse to take it.

Recovery, on the other hand, is about investing in your future. Robert Louis Stevenson said, "Don't judge each day by the harvest you reap, but by the seeds that you plant." So let's list a few of the seeds you can plant, which will bear fruit in the days to come.

- Sponsor someone in recovery.
- Volunteer to tutor.
- Join a civic club.
- Read my daily Recovery Minute email.
- Memorize the 7th Step Prayer.
- Meet someone from your group for lunch or dinner.

At first, long-term sobriety feels foreign. Thomas Carlyle was right: "Every noble work is at first impossible." Then it becomes manageable. Eventually, possible. But it will never happen unless you get started. Plant some seeds of recovery. Then step back and wait. What you planted today, God will harvest tomorrow.

RULE #34

Direction trumps destination.

"Change your direction and you change your destiny."
Mark Victor Hansen

If you start off toward the moon, but are off by just one percent, you'll miss it by thousands of miles. If your drive on the golf course is off just a little, by the time it stops rolling, it will be either wet or in the sand.

In recovery, don't think too much about your destination. Focus on direction instead. I have found that when I seek answers, I come up empty. But when I seek God, the answers find me. So seek the God of the universe. Trust the Holy Spirit to keep your recovery on track, as long as you are walking with him.

Perhaps you need a change of direction. Here are just a few things you can do today that will change your destiny tomorrow.

1. Conclude that something must change.
2. Connect with healthy people.
3. Create a plan of action.
4. Choose to take action.

In other words, make your focus the direction in which you know you should be heading. Then start off in that direction. If you do that, the destination will take care of itself.

RULE #35

Relapse does not equal failure; quitting does.

"Persistence conquers all things."
Benjamin Franklin

In 1941, Winston Churchill addressed the students at the Harrow School in England, during the darkest days of World War II. Among his comments were the famous words, "Never give in, never give up. Never, never, never." His words were given to encourage the British in their war with Germany.

We are all in a war – for integrity, sobriety, and recovery. And no one does recovery perfectly. We have all had our share of slips, relapses, and setbacks. The key is to never give up. The only people I know who have failed in recovery are the ones who quit too soon. Everyone else has made it.

I have learned a few things about how to stay in the battle, to never give up.

1. Learn from each fall. Never let a relapse go to waste. Make every setback your personal tutor. Learn from it, and move on.
2. Adjust your course. Remember, your current strategy is perfectly suited for the results you are getting. So if you fall, after you get up, do something different going forward.

3. Create a schedule. Strategies to stay sober are useless – unless they come with a schedule. *When* will you see a therapist? *When* will you go to your next meeting? *When* will you do your disclosure? *When* will you do a Recovery Day? *When* will you start working the 12 Steps?
4. Develop one new habit. Start small. Do something new each day that you can stick with. It might be a short devotional time, physical exercise, journaling, or daily calls.
5. Remember the end game. Always remind yourself of how things end up with each relapse – the guilt, shame, embarrassment, and loss.

Every person I know who has long-term sobriety got there by persistence. I like the way Bill Bradley said it. "Ambition is the path to success, and persistence is the vehicle you arrive in." Get on board with persistence. It will take you where you want to go.

RULE #36

Recovery is 10 percent what happens to you and 90 percent what happens in you.

"It's not what happens to you, but how you react that matters."
Epictetus

We all have had our share of trauma. And abuse. And pain. And resentment. The list goes on and on. No one asked to be an addict. No one signs up for this. In a sense, we are all victims. But you can only play that card for so long. Eventually, you have to own your disease. If you were neglected as a child, that's on your parents. But if you took a drink this morning, that's on you. Every relapse is a choice.

What happens *to* you matters. But what happens *in* you matters more. And you get a voice in that.

We've all said it . . .

If I had gotten the job promotion . . .
If I had been picked for the team . . .
If I had lived in a better place . . .
If my parents had taken me to church . . .
If I was a little taller . . .
If I was a little thinner . . .
If I had a little more money . . .

Get that out of your system. "If I" doesn't help. It only serves to remind you of past pain. I think I have a better plan. Ask yourself these questions instead.

What can I learn from this?
How can I do things differently next time?
How can I pray for the person who hurt me?
How can this make me a better person?
How can I use this to help someone else?
What was my part in this?
If God is for me, who can stand against me?

RULE #37

If you aren't working on your recovery, you're working on your relapse.

"Grow or die. There's no such thing as stagnant."
Dustin Stout

Nothing that is alive remains stagnant. Trees, vegetables, fruits – they are growing or they are dying. Your growth and recovery will continue until the day you die. If you are reading this, you are probably not dead yet. So keep learning, growing, and changing.

"If it ain't broke, don't fix it."

I hate that phrase. Everything is in a state of decay. Every building, machine, and person. It's not a matter of being "broke." It's a matter of growth.

Henry Ford said, "Anyone who stops learning is old, whether at twenty or eighty. Anyone who keeps learning stays young."

I want to stay young. That requires daily upkeep and growth, new relationships, and new adventures.

Let me ask you a few questions . . .

What was the last book you read about recovery?
Who was the last person you sponsored?
When was the last time you listened to a recovery podcast?
What are you doing today that you weren't doing a year ago?

How will you grow in your recovery this week?

There are a lot of ways to grow in our recovery. There are new groups, therapists, tools, books, podcasts, websites, blogs, and lectures to take advantage of. There are conferences and Recovery Days. There are new exercise programs, meditation guides, and places to hike. There is no limit to the resources available – if you want them.

Let me say it again. You are either working on your recovery today, or you are working on your relapse. The thing is, by doing nothing, you are actually doing something. Whatever works today will fade tomorrow. Yes, we need the consistency of the same group every week, year after year. But we need more than that. God is the God of a new song, new thing, and new day. Open yourself to the possibility there is something you can do for your recovery today that you never did before.

RULE #38

One of the best ways to secure your own sobriety is to help someone else secure theirs.

"Having had a spiritual awakening as the result of these steps, we tried to carry this message to alcoholics, and to practice these principles in all our affairs."
Step 12, Alcoholics Anonymous

Recovery is the one thing you get more of as you give it away. And it's never too early to start. I remember my second 12-Step meeting. A young man identified himself as new to the group. When the meeting was over, I walked over to him and encouraged him, giving him free literature, exchanging cell numbers, and offering to help him in any way that I could. I had almost nothing to offer him at that time, but I didn't know that! There was just something inside of me screaming, "Help this dude!" I can't tell you the great feeling I had as I left that meeting. My recovery took a giant leap forward as I helped my new friend take a tiny step forward in his own recovery.

A recent study from Columbia University confirms the power of helping others. Over a three-week period, participants in the study were provided an anonymous online platform on which they could share their struggles and stress points. The others on the platform could then respond to each other, with suggestions and advice. The study found that at the end of the three weeks, the people who had offered the most help to others were happier and more satisfied with their lives than the ones who actually received the help. On the other hand, the people who only posted their needs, but offered no help to others, ended the period in a more depressed state than they were in before the study began.

St. Francis of Assisi was right: "It is in the giving that we receive."

This week, if you want to secure your own sobriety, help someone else to secure theirs. Offer to take someone to lunch. Pray for them. Send them points of encouragement. Sit with them at the next meeting. Introduce them to others in your group. Provide resources at your own expense. Don't let the week pass without helping yourself – by helping someone else.

RULE #39

You're probably spending too much time on social media.

"It takes discipline to not let social media steal your time."
Alexis Ohanian

As of this writing, there are 4.76 billion social media users in the world, which accounts for 59.4 percent of the population. The average person on social media spends 2 hours and 31 minutes on social media each day. That is more time than they spend in prayer, Bible reading, eating, exercise, with their family, and on their hobbies – combined.

So I'll repeat Rule #39 – You're probably spending too much time on social media.

Brene Brown writes, "Social media has given us this idea that we should all have a posse of friends when in reality, if we have one or two really good friends, we are lucky."

Columbia professors Claude Mellins and Deborah Glasofer conducted extensive psychotherapy development research for adults who struggle with behavioral addictions. They found ten negative effects that result from social media use.

1. Reduced face-to-face interaction
2. Increased cravings for attention
3. Distraction from life goals

4. Higher risk of depression
5. Failed relationships
6. Stunted creativity
7. Encounters with cyberbullies
8. Reduced self-esteem
9. Loss of sleep (Duh!)
10. Lack of privacy

I heard someone say, "The greatest example that we could be spending more time in prayer is the amount of time we waste on social media each day." Now, I'm not saying you should quit social media altogether. But I can tell you I got off social media a decade ago, and have not missed it a bit. That's because I've replaced it with this thing we call – a life!

Yep, you're probably spending too much time on social media.

RULE #40

One step taken is better than 1,000 steps planned.

"Life is what happens to you while you're planning on doing something else."
John Lennon

I am the world's #1 best planner. I plan everything, every day. I plan my schedule in 15-minute increments, one week in advance. That includes when I'll exercise, eat breakfast, work, etc. Everything. I plan my budget. Then I plan a new budget. I love to plan. And don't even think about going on a vacation with us unless you are committed to the agenda.

I exaggerate a bit, but not much. I love to plan. And that's good. I learned a long time ago that if you aim at nothing, you'll hit it every time. You need to plan. That is especially true with recovery. Lasting sobriety is the natural result of meetings, calls, session, books, podcasts, Step work, and more. And none of these things just happen. They have to be planned.

But planning is not enough. All planning does is get you to the starting line. Leadership expert Peter Drucker said, "Plans are only good intentions unless they immediately degenerate into hard work."

Dad taught me the value of hard work. I'm so glad that he did. When I look around, I'm shocked at how many lazy people there are in the world. When I lost my ministry at the end of 2014, we moved to Florida to be near our son. My wife always said she didn't worry about money because she knew I was a hard worker. But I had no idea what I'd do when we got to Florida. I had no clue that we would ever launch a recovery ministry at that time. For me, recovery was new and doubts were high.

So what did I do? I made a plan. And then I worked that plan. In our early years in Florida, I put my doctorate, 31 years of pastoring, and other credentials on the shelf, and I shifted. I did the following jobs, many of them simultaneously: Uber driver, Lyft driver, Shipt grocery deliveries, driving old people to doctor appointments, funerals, airport transport, proofreading, and various writing projects.

Recovery is the hardest job I've ever had. It never takes a day off. There are devotions to read, Steps to work, calls to make, sponsees to lead, and meetings to attend. You need a recovery plan. But what you really need is recovery *work*.

RULE #41

The best recovery group is the one you actually show up to.

"The Church is a group of people ordained from Heaven to operate on God's behalf."
Tony Evans

I can't overstate the value of attending recovery groups. If I didn't believe in groups, our ministry wouldn't offer so many of them. At any given time, we have ten or more recovery groups going. I lead groups for pastors, doctors, couples, and any men who struggle with unwanted sexual behaviors. As part of my training for my Master's in addiction recovery, I was required to attend six Alcoholics Anonymous meetings. (I don't drink.)

But I've seen it too many times. Men and women who struggle with addictions have a bigger problem – paralysis by analysis. It's easy to overthink it. We can find something wrong with any group. It's too far away, the meetings are too long, they are too faith-based, they are not enough faith-based, the curriculum stinks, and the leader seems clueless.

Here's what I do to overcome all of that. Before my weekly 12-Step meeting, which I have attended faithfully since 2014, I pray a simple prayer: "Let me hear one thing tonight that I can use." And every time I pray that prayer, I don't leave disappointed.

There is no perfect group. (If there was, you'd mess it up by showing up!) But I have found a really good group. It's the group I actually decide to attend. Don't let the perfect become the enemy of the good. You can shop around for a group if you want to. But land on one quickly. Get a sponsor, become a sponsor, jump in and help.

There are 62,397 reasons to join a group. Let me give you just five of those reasons.

1. Groups provide hope. In each group you will hear stories of other addicts who have found sobriety. In their stories there is hope.
2. Groups provide accountability. Each week, you will check in. That means confessing any slips or relapses. Accountability is critical to recovery.
3. Groups provide friendships. I'd guess that 90 percent of my friends are in recovery groups. Why not? We share so much in common.
4. Groups are practical. There is nothing more practical or systematic than working the 12 Steps. My Freedom Groups offer great practicality, as well.
5. Groups move you forward. By sharing life with others in recovery, you will find a path forward. Nothing is better than that.

RULE #42

An ugly truth beats a pretty lie.

"A liar will not be believed, even when he's telling the truth."
Aesop

Sometimes, the truth is very painful. I didn't like it when my doctor said I needed glasses at age eight, that I needed eye surgery at 19, or that I needed open heart surgery at 62. But an ugly truth beats a pretty lie. Would I have been better off if my doctors had told me what I hoped to hear? Of course not.

Sometimes, the truth hurts. But a lie is worse. You can be in recovery or you can be dishonest. But you can't be both.

Addicts are good at one thing – lying. It comes from years of practice. Now, don't misunderstand. Addicts don't always tell what we call "bold-faced lies." That would be too obvious. Instead, addicts tell half-truths. Much of what they say is true; the goal is that you'll buy it all. But as Benjamin Franklin said, "A half truth is a whole lie."

What is wrong with telling lies, exactly? The obvious answer is that it destroys trust and relationships. But I came across an interesting study reported by Dr. Bella Depaulo, a psychologist at the University of Virginia. Dr. Depaulo cites a project conducted by University College in London, in which participants were told to study a jar of pennies, then state how many pennies they guessed were in that jar. They were told that if they overestimated the number, they would be granted a reward.

When they began exaggerating the number of pennies in the jar, their amygdala, the brain's built-in gauge of right and wrong, responded to their dishonesty, with feelings of guilt and stress. But with each exaggeration, the reaction within the brain lessened. Dr. Depaulo concluded, "When we lie for personal gain, our amygdala produces a negative feeling that limits the extent to which we are prepared to lie. But that feeling fades, and the lies become bigger."

Conclusion: The biggest problem with lying is not the damage it does to the person to whom we lie, but the damage it does to the person telling the lie.

RULE #43

You are what you continually do.

"You are what you do, not what you say you'll do."
Carl Jung

Every action changes the person who takes that action. Think about it. Eat a cupcake, and that changes you. You become just a tad less healthy. Run a mile, and that changes you for the better, assuming you don't die in the process. But here's where we get off track. We all *plan* to do better. We *intend* to stay sober. We *strive* to stay clean. But *plan*, *intend*, and *strive* won't cut it. You have to actually *do* those things.

Have you noticed that you tend to judge others by their actions, but you judge yourself by your intentions? You *meant* to stay sober, cut off the affair, or stay out of the bar. I hate to tell you this, but you're using the wrong scoreboard!

Researchers James Prochaska and Carlo DiClemente have created the Stages of Change model, which suggests that there are periods we must go through to change who we are. With each change comes a new revelation and breakthrough.

- Stage 1 – Precontemplation. Yes, this is a stage of change. This is when you say, "I don't really have a problem. I can stop drinking anytime." But the key is you're at least thinking about it.

- Stage 2 – Contemplation. Now, you realize you have a problem. Your drug use is affecting your performance. Your video game use has gotten out of hand. Your spending is costing you dearly.
- Stage 3 – Preparation. You start the research. You look for a therapist. You read some books on addiction. Prochaska says that 50 percent of those who skip this stage will relapse within 21 days.
- Stage 4 – Action. Not just any action will do. It is action that follows good preparation that produces the best results. In this stage, you follow a detailed plan for recovery. This may include therapy, groups, and a disclosure.
- Stage 5 – Maintenance. Through action, new habits are established. Through maintenance, they become second nature. The problem with recovery is that it leaks. If you don't maintain new recovery routines, your recovery will become perilous.

RULE #44

Recovery never takes a day off.

"The reward for work well done is the opportunity to do more."
Jonas Salk

Most projects allow for a day off every now and then. In fact, it is a good thing to take a day off. That's why God created this thing called the Sabbath. We need rest. It's important to recharge at the end of each week.

There is one exception – *recovery*.

Why does recovery never get a day off? Because your addiction never takes a day off. Addiction doesn't follow a calendar and take a break for weekends and holidays. If the enemy is going to punch you in the face every day, you need to be prepared to respond – every day.

Demi Lovato said it like this: "Recovery is something that you have to work on every single day and it's something that doesn't get a day off."

I believe this so much that I wrote the only 365-day devotional book for sex addicts that I know of. I write a daily Recovery Minute devotional that is read in 25 countries. My 90-day recovery program requires daily readings and exercises. My one-year Life Recovery Plan includes daily readings and weekly exercises.

Until the enemy takes a day off, you don't get a day off. So let me suggest some things you can do to maintain your recovery – every day.

- Say the Serenity Prayer.
- Say the 3rd Step Prayer.
- Say the 7th Step Prayer.
- Read one paragraph of recovery material.
- Make contact with one other person in recovery.
- Exercise for a few minutes.
- Read Scripture.

Come up with your own list. Find your own rhythm. Do the things that work for you. The key is not to do a ton of recovery work every week, but to do a little each day.

RULE #45

You don't need to see the entire staircase to take the next step.

"Take one step toward me. I will meet you there."
God

"Just as I am, without one plea,
But that Thy blood was shed for me.
And that Thou bid'st me come to Thee,
Oh, Lamb of God, I come. I come."

We've been singing that old hymn since Charlotte Elliot wrote it in 1835. While Elliot wrote 125 other hymns, none of them is notable. But one was enough.

God says to take one step toward him, and he'll take it from there. Come just as you are, without one plea, but that his blood was shed for thee.

First steps are huge.

I took my first step into College Park Baptist Church in August 1973. It was there that I would meet my Savior. On April 15, 1979, I took my first step into First Baptist Church of Genoa, in Houston, as Student Pastor. It was there that I would meet my wife. On May 26, 1990, I took my first step into the delivery room at Methodist Hospital in Houston. It was there that I met my son.

But my scariest first step came in 2013. I stepped into the noon Sex Addicts Anonymous meeting at Bering Memorial United Methodist Church in Houston. It was there that I found recovery.

Rarely do we know what will come after that first step. I had no idea what was at the top of that staircase. If I knew all that would follow, I might have stayed in my car. But that's how recovery works. Just take the first step. After that, take one more step. You don't need to see the top of the staircase to take the next step.

What is your first step? You've already taken it, or you wouldn't be reading this. So what's your next step? A meeting? A call? A session? A book? If you seek, you will find. God is not in the business of hiding recovery from you. So go ahead. Take the next step. The rest can come later.

RULE #46

You can collect chips, but you can't check boxes.

"My unfaithful husband checked all the boxes. But none of it was real."
"Wendy"

Chips, yes. Boxes, no. Let me explain. We'll start with chips. Most 12-Step recovery groups offer chips to mark dates of recovery, measured in months, and then years. Nothing wrong with that. I'm happy to collect a new chip from my own group each year. Chips matter, because they represent progress.

Now let's talk about boxes. We all know what it means to check boxes. When we shop for groceries, we check off each item from our list as it is placed in the cart. Our daily agenda has boxes to check. Once the task is completed, we check the box. Checking boxes is representative of task completion.

And it has no place in recovery.

I have known a few addicts who have made a case that their addiction has simply gone away. In each case I either (a) don't believe them, or (b) feel sorry for them. In some cases, I don't believe them, because their lifestyle contradicts their words. In other cases, when they make a plausible case, I feel sorry for them, because now they have to find something else to keep them humble, surrendered, and on guard.

A study in 2019 found that, on average, a person finds lasting recovery after five failures. The same study found that people who experienced lasting sobriety were better at coping with life's challenges than those who had no addiction at all. They concluded this was because a person who actively does recovery work is more balanced, prepared, and alert.

Chips mark milestones. Boxes mark completion. Milestones are a good thing. Completion is not. Even if you could get beyond "addict" status, I don't know why you'd want to! It is addiction that brought you to recovery, and it is recovery that has brought you the serenity that most people outside of recovery only dream of.

RULE #47

If all you do is what you've done, all you'll get is what you've got.

"If you do not change direction,
you may end up where you are heading."
Lao Tzu

Recovery is active, not passive. It doesn't just happen. In fact, the opposite is true. If you don't pursue recovery every day, you'll lose ground. Recovery is a hill to climb, not conquer. And on that climb, you will need to change things up from time to time, especially if you aren't making much progress.

A friend in recovery told me recently, "I don't understand why I can't get much traction. I stay sober for a month or two, then fall back into old habits." I asked him about his program. It was solid – weekly meetings, daily calls, and Step work. So what was the problem? The problem was that he was treating pneumonia as if he had a head cold. He needed to do more, at least in the short run.

My favorite physician was a man named Dr. Seuss. While I'm not sure where he went to medical school, the guy was brilliant. He offered this nugget of truth: "You have brains in your head. You have feet in your shoes. You can steer yourself in any direction you choose. You're on your own, and you know what to do. And you are the guy who'll decide where to go."

I love that. We are in control of our recovery. If your finances are a wreck, blame it on the economy. If your job stinks, blame it on your boss. If your team is losing, blame it on your coach. But if your recovery is tanking, blame it on yourself.

But there is hope. Lara Galinsky, an expert on making changes that redirect our future, has suggested three steps to making a major course change.

1. Identify. Take time to isolate the problem. Why is your recovery slacking? What is the missing piece to your weekly program? What is behind the relapses?
2. Prioritize. Make a list of the things you need to change, and put them in order of importance. Your list may be long, but your priorities should not be. Isolate two or three things you can do immediately to improve your program.
3. Solve. Get to work. Go all in with your new plan. No excuses. No delays. No distraction. If you value your sanity, marriage, and walk with God, you will do what you know to do. Remember, if all you do is what's you've done, then all you'll get is what you've got.

RULE #48

When your past calls, let it go to voicemail.

"You can't change the past, but you can ruin the present by worrying about it."
Isak Dinesen

I have this guy who keeps calling me on my cell phone. I don't know how he got my number, but he is really persistent. I see his name come up on my phone, so I know it's him. We've never met, and I'm a busy person, so I let his calls go to voicemail. His name is "Spam."

We all have a lot of spam in our lives. Spam comes in many forms. Spam may be a TV show we should walk away from. It may be a website we should avoid. Spam even comes in the form of people who are annoying and demanding. Sometimes we need to send Spam to voicemail.

That's what Nehemiah did. Remember when he was building the wall around Jerusalem? A couple of fellows named Sanballat and Tobiah kept trying to engage him in meaningless conversation. He finally told them to take a long walk on a short pier. He didn't have time for their nonsense.

Neither do you. Time is short. (You can quote me on that.) You don't have time for Spam. One of the greatest examples of Spam is your past. It will come calling; you can count on that. Your past will call you up and say, "You're no good." Or it may say, "You can't stay sober." My past will tell me, "Old habits will return." I've learned that there is only one good response when my past calls.

Let it go to voicemail.

Charles Swindoll writes, "We cannot change the past. We can't change the fact that people act in a certain way. We can't change the inevitable. The only thing we can do is play on the one string we have, and that is our attitude."

We overcome the past with a forward-looking attitude. We learn from our past, but we can't live there.

B.K. Geeta, writing for *The Daily Guardian*, offers a helpful observation. "If we are burdened by the past and it stops us from doing what we need to do in the present, we are setting ourselves up for more sorrow and disappointment." Amen to that! The next time your past calls, treat it like Spam. Let it go to voicemail.

RULE #49

Nothing matters more than surrender.

"We humbly asked God to remove all our shortcomings."
Step 7, Alcoholics Anonymous

"All to Jesus I surrender,
All to Him I freely give.
I will ever love and trust Him,
In His presence daily live.

"All to Jesus I surrender,
Humbly at His feet I bow.
Worldly pleasures all forsaken,
Take me Jesus, take me now.

"I surrender all.
I surrender all.
All to Thee, my blessed Savior,
I surrender all."

I was raised on that great hymn, written by an art teacher named Judson Van DeVenter in 1896. But I've learned that singing "I Surrender All" is a whole lot easier than living it. It's not that I don't surrender everything to God. The problem is that I do so with sticky hands. I never really let it go. I keep pulling things back.

There are a lot of things that matter in recovery – going to meetings, making calls, doing therapy, working the Steps, finding a sponsor. But what matters most is not what we do, but what we give. We must surrender all.

We need to be like the little boy at church. When it came time for the offering, the pastor implored the people to give all they could to the Lord that day. Then they passed the offering plate. When the plate got to this little boy, he put the plate on the floor and stepped into it. "What are you doing?" asked the usher. "I'm doing what the preacher said!" replied the boy. "I'm giving God all that I can. I'm giving him me."

The old poem says it well. "What can I give him, small as I am? If I were a shepherd, I'd give him a lamb. If I were a wise man, I'd surely do my part. But what can I give him? I can give him my heart." That's surrender. And it's a prerequisite for good recovery.

RULE #50

Make every setback your personal tutor.

"A man who asks is a fool for five minutes. A man who never asks is a fool for life."
Chinese Proverb

A setback is only a failure if you don't learn from it. In my first year of recovery, I defined "setback." I struggled to get a month of sobriety. Part of the reason was that I didn't come into recovery of my own accord. It was a discovery that my wife made that gave me no choice. I wanted to be sober, but not badly enough to seek it on my own.

But now I had no choice. Like most, it was a crisis that thrust me into 12-Step meetings and recovery work. And like most, the first year was pretty rocky. But looking back, it wasn't a total loss. That's because with every setback, a lesson was learned. Relapses can teach you things that can't be learned any other way. I'm not saying you should have a relapse – ever. But remember that anything God allows (even bad stuff), he will redeem.

In order for your setback to be your personal tutor, you need to ask yourself two questions.

First, ask yourself, *"What was I doing?"* Were you going to the wrong places, hanging with the wrong crowd, indulging in the wrong habits? Were you living in the middle circle, the danger zone? Relapse doesn't just happen. Remember, it is a process, not an event. So when you have a setback, you need to ask yourself what you were doing in the last 24 hours and the last 24 minutes that set you up for the fall.

Second, ask yourself, *"What was I not doing?"* Perhaps you were not going to meetings. Maybe you missed your daily devotional time for several days. Or it could be that you became lax in recovery readings and Step work. You took your foot off the pedal. You put the car in neutral. It's not that you were out looking for trouble. But you don't need to look for trouble; it will find you. And when it does, if you are doing nothing to stay sober, you'll be a sitting duck.

Don't plan for setbacks. But when and if they come, listen to them. Learn from them. Your setbacks are great tutors. Never miss a good opportunity to learn from a bad experience.

RULE #51

None of us is as strong as all of us.

*"We need each other. The sooner we learn that,
the better for us all."*
Erik Erikson

According to research from the National Academies of Sciences, Engineering, and Medicine, "More than one-third of adults aged 45 and older feel lonely, and nearly one-fourth of adults aged 65 and older are considered to be socially isolated." The CDC notes that such isolation can have serious health effects, including a 50 percent increased risk for dementia, heart disease, and stroke. They find that isolation also affects our mental health, leading to increased risk for depression, anxiety, and even suicide.

Add addiction into the mix and you have a recipe for disaster. That's where connection comes in. Connection is the antidote to addiction. You can seek recovery without connection, and you'll get neither. Or you can seek connection with recovery and get both.

My friend Dennis Swanberg has created a model for how this works. He calls it "The Man Code." It is a simple formula for connection that was modeled by Jesus and that works today. We need certain numbers in our lives.

- 1 – This is God.
- 3 – Peter, James, and John. This represents an inner circle of people of your same sex, who know your struggles and help to hold you accountable.
- 12 – Jesus' disciples. This represents a small group, support group, or 12-Step group.
- 120 – This was the number of the early church in Jerusalem. You need to be in a church, the Body of Christ.
- 5,000 – The men Jesus fed. This number represents your broader community. You need to be plugged in to the lives of neighbors, associates, and others outside of your church and small group.

You can do recovery alone, but it won't go well. That's not because you aren't strong enough or smart enough. It's because that's not how you were designed by the Creator. Doing recovery on your own is like unpacking a huge piece of furniture, then tossing away the directions that were written by the manufacturer, as if you know more than they do. According to your Manufacturer, you were created for community. None of us is as strong as all of us.

RULE #52

You don't realize Jesus is all you need until Jesus is all you have.

"Apart from him we can do nothing
because we have in us no life."
A.T. Pierson

There are numerous prayers in the Book of Psalms worthy of repeating to God. Here's one of them, found in Psalm 73:25-26.

"Whom have I in heaven but you? And there is nothing on earth that I desire besides you. My flesh and my heart may fail, but God is the strength of my heart and my portion forever."

When people ask Beth what it took to give me another chance, she says, "Mark was out of chances. What it came down to for me was whether I was willing to give God another chance."

Jesus told a story about a man who sold everything he had in order to find a seemingly worthless field, because in that field was buried treasure. Think of that treasure as recovery and the field as God. When you lose everything else, you still have the field and the treasure that he provides. And that is enough.

I lay in the hospital in Sarasota, Florida, on the night of November 10, 2022. I knew that in a few hours, at 4:30 a.m., nurses would awaken me to begin the process of preparation for surgery. I had spent the last five days in the hospital, knowing this day would come. I had had a major heart attack, and if my heart would gain enough strength, I'd be facing a five-bypass open heart surgery. On Day 5, my heart regained enough strength to undergo surgery. As I tried to sleep late that night, no one else was in the room. It was just me and God. And that was enough.

Randy Alcorn says that God is *not* enough. But he explains that when he looks down on us in our deepest need, he provides that which we need. So he is the instrument of our provision. In other words, when Jesus is all you have, Jesus is all you need.

RULE #53

Today's level of sobriety was the predictable outcome of what you did yesterday.

"Everything you do today will impact your tomorrow."
Frank Sonnenberg

When I was early in my recovery, I remember going to 12-Step meetings and sitting in awe as men collected chips marking 30 days, six months, and one year of recovery. When one guy picked up his 10-year chip, I looked at him like he was a unicorn. How was this even possible? In my covetous state, it seemed like the "chip gods" randomly selected those to whom they would impart chips. I'd look at the guy who got his 3-year chip and think, "How lucky is that guy?"

It turns out there are no "chip gods."

If you have six months of sobriety, there's a reason for that. If you have five years, there's a reason for that. And if you only have a couple of days of sobriety, there's a reason for that, too. Your sobriety (or lack thereof) is the predictable result of what you did yesterday. And last week.

How do you achieve your goals for sobriety? Entrepreneur Warren Rustand offers three steps that he has seen work hundreds of times.

Step 1 – Intent is not enough.

Plans are good, but they are not enough. Intending to stay sober is not staying sober. You've heard of the log with five frogs on it? If three decided to jump off, how many frogs would remain on the log? Answer: five. Deciding to jump and actually jumping are not the same thing.

Step 2 – Link, align, connect.

Your intent must be linked, aligned, and connected to a plan of action. There must be a specific strategy that transforms your intentions into a means to carry that out.

Step 3 – Disciplined actions drive outcomes.

You need actions that align with your recovery intents. But not just any actions. Discipline is the key. It is the consistency of doing the same thing every day that brings success.

RULE #54

Revisit your three circles every three months.

"We draw three concentric circles, consisting of the inner, middle, and outer circle."
Alcoholics Anonymous

You are probably familiar with the three circles. Here's a quick review. Take a sheet of paper and draw a large circle. Then draw a smaller circle inside of the first circle. Finally, draw a smaller circle in the center. The outer circle represents recovery activities. The middle circle includes anything that puts your sobriety in jeopardy. And the inner circle contains anything that breaks your sobriety.

Now, write several words in each circle, on the sheet of paper. You will essentially be making a list of the things that keep you in a good place, the things that should be avoided when possible, and that which resets your sobriety date.

Doing this exercise is a great way to get entrenched in a strong recovery program. But the mistake most of us make is that we complete the exercise, then walk away from it. We don't even remember what we put in each circle. But even that is not enough. If you want to keep your recovery on track, review your circles every few months. See If anything needs to be shifted or added to one of the circles.

This requires self-reflection. Dr. Tchiki Davis addresses this in her article, "What Is Self-Reflection and Why It Matters for Wellness." Dr. Davis suggests that through self-reflection we identify weaknesses in our lives that need to be addressed. But that's only the beginning. "The next step is to cultivate the desire to change behaviors that bother you. After identifying any problematic aspects of yourself, take the wheel and slowly shift your behavior in ways that better represent how you want to be."

As you do this exercise, focus largely on your middle circle. The inner circle activities may never change. You pretty much know what acts constitute a loss of sobriety. The same goes for the outer circle. You know what belongs there. These things don't shift around much. But the middle circle may need to be updated from time to time. Revisit your circles every three months.

RULE #55

The more you have, the less you trust.

"It is easier for a camel to go through the eye of a needle than for a rich person to enter the Kingdom of God."
Jesus

What usually drives a person into recovery is a significant loss or threat of a loss. The opposite is also true. Far too often, when things are going well, we see addicts showing up in meetings disguised as empty chairs. Their recovery work becomes lax, as they are less motivated to work as hard as before.

Jesus said that a camel is more likely to pass through the eye of a needle than a rich man is to pass into the Kingdom of God. His point was that when life is easy, we become far less likely to let God run our lives.

The American mindset is that prosperity equals God's favor. Vicky Banks writes on this subject, asking the question, "Why is it so hard to trust God?" She writes, "I was only viewing the trustworthiness of God and of his Word through the lens of my circumstances, when I should have been viewing my circumstances through the lens of God's unchanging Word."

While we might think having money would lead people to just kick back and enjoy life, that's not true. A survey conducted by the University of Chicago found that if they won the lottery, 70 percent of Americans would continue to work. We know, intuitively, that money is not enough.

Let's broaden that out a bit. Some addicts just can't stand prosperity. They self-sabotage, because they have an inherent need to live in dependence on God in order to stay sober. If you are doing really well financially, that's great! But be careful. Don't let what you own become more important to you than what you need.

RULE #56

No man can serve two masters.

"The man who is popular with the world is not a friend of Jesus."
D.L. Moody

Focus is a huge part of recovery. Jesus said we can't serve two masters at the same time (Matthew 6:24-26). And his brother James said a double-minded man is in constant trouble (James 1:8). In our spiritual lives as well as in our addiction recovery, we must keep our eye on the prize.

I read about an interesting study of how most people have little idea of their basic activities pertaining to health. On average, we underestimate the number of calories we are really taking in, by 47 percent. And we overestimate our level of daily physical activity by 51 percent.

I suspect the same holds true for recovery. Most of us probably think we do more recovery work than we really do. But we get distracted, forget to pray, miss a few meetings, and relax our habits. In other words, we lose focus. Like a driver distracted by too many things off the road, we can swerve if we don't stay focused.

Let me suggest three keys to staying focused on your recovery.

1. Develop a daily agenda. My daily agenda includes praying the 3rd Step Prayer, 7th Step Prayer, and Serenity Prayer, as

well as one paragraph of recovery reading. This rigid discipline does not guarantee I'll succeed with my recovery, but to not have an agenda will nearly guarantee that I'll fail.

2. Avoid all middle circle activities all the time. Treat your middle circle like it's your inner circle. Avoid going there at all costs. To think you can dabble in the middle circle and never fall would be like jumping off a tall building, thinking you won't eventually hit the ground.

3. Read two new recovery books each year. This will keep your recovery fresh. Remember, recovery leaks. It is critical to keep growing, keep learning, and keep moving forward.

RULE #57

The unexamined life is not worth living.

"For my part, whatever anguish of spirit it may cost,
I am willing to know the whole truth;
to know the worst and to provide for it."
Dana Reeve

It is one of the iconic statements in the history of Christendom. "The unexamined life is not worth living." That quote is originally attributed to Socrates at his trial for supposedly corrupting the youth with his philosophy. His words represent his view of death, as he would be martyred for his beliefs.

The same is true for any addict who seeks long-term sobriety. Any unexamined recovery is not worth having. We should constantly review our recovery work with humility and willingness to change. Bill W., the founder of AA, wrote, "For the wise have always known that no one can make much of his life until self-searching has become a regular habit, until he is able to admit and accept what he finds, and until he patiently and persistently tries to correct what is wrong."

What does it mean to examine one's recovery? It means asking ourselves the hard questions. Give yourself ten points for each question you answer positively.

- Am I further along in my recovery than I was this time last year?
- Am I truly sober, or am I just technically sober today?
- Am I really doing recovery work, or just checking the boxes?
- Have I intentionally helped someone else in their recovery this month?
- Have I been completely honest with my sponsor and/or group?
- Have I shared all my secrets with my spouse or trusted friend?
- Am I getting good exercise, eating wisely, and getting enough sleep?
- Do I serve at my local church?
- Do I maintain good guardrails?
- Do I generally stay out of my middle circle?

If you scored 70 or above, you are probably in a pretty good place with your recovery. But don't stop now. Keep moving forward, and keep asking yourself the hard questions.

RULE #58

Pray, not to find answers, but to find God.

"The function of prayer is not to influence God, but rather to change the nature of the one who prays."
Soren Kierkegaard

If you're like me (let's hope not, for your sake), you pray selfishly. "God, heal me. Give me that job I want. Meet my needs. And my desires. Give me, give me, give me."

But true prayer is about seeking the God of blessings, rather than the blessings of God. And when we do that, heaven and earth are moved. D.L. Moody observed, "Every great movement of God can be traced to a kneeling figure."

We seek God in prayer. But we find God in other ways. Here are a few examples.

1. Pain. C.S. Lewis said that anyone who thinks nothing good comes from pain has never been to a dentist. He wrote, in *The Problem of Pain*, "God whispers to us in our pleasures, speaks in our consciences, but shouts in our pain. It is his megaphone to rouse a deaf world."

2. Move. Get outdoors, go somewhere different, look for a new experience. In Exodos 33, we read that Moses went outside the camp to seek the Lord. This was a conscious choice to find God in a unique way.

3. Confess. The prophet said our sin would separate us from God, so that he cannot hear our prayers (Isaiah 59:2). Keep your record clean every day. Confess what you know you've done, thought, and said that was not pleasing to God.

4. Gratitude. In everything give thanks (1 Thessalonians 5:18). With a grateful spirit you experience God in a fresh way.

5. Surrender. It is God who orders our steps (Jeremiah 10:23). To find God, you must surrender to him. Surrender your possessions, thoughts, and heart. Give him your time, your talent, and your treasure.

Recovery is not transactional. We don't do something in particular in order to be given sobriety as some kind of tradeoff. The real blessing is not the sobriety we seek, but the journey we walk. One of the truisms I have found in my life is that when I seek answers, I find frustration. But when I seek God, the answers find me. So keep praying – to find God.

RULE #59

Recovery leaks.

*"It is the inconsequential leak
which empties the biggest reservoir."*
Charles Comiskey

I remember sitting in a huge leadership conference in Chicago years ago. I was in awe of the host church, the largest church in America at that time. I was blown away by all the speakers and the entire experience. But I only remember one line from all the messages, spread over three days.

"Vision leaks."

The point was that leaders need to constantly recast their vision for their church, business, or organization. Otherwise, people forget the vision, their goals become murky, and the organization loses focus.

The same is true with recovery. It leaks. What you did yesterday will carry you through today, but not tomorrow. What you learned in your therapy session last week was great, but you can't stop learning now. What you gleaned from your last 12-Step meeting was helpful, but it will only carry you so far. Why?

Recovery leaks.

John Bunyan said, "One leak will sink a ship, and one sin will destroy a sinner." If Bunyan were writing this lesson on recovery, I think he would say something like this.

"It doesn't matter how solid your recovery ship is if it has one leak. You can go to meetings, do the work, make the calls, and read the books. But if you don't plug the leak, you'll eventually drown. That leak may be a trigger you haven't addressed. It may be a relationship you need to end. It may be a habit that must be conquered. One leak. That's all it takes to sink your ship."

I agree with John Bunyan! One leak will sink your ship. Yes, you need to keep doing the things that work. But never take recovery for granted. If you try to just cruise in your recovery, your ship will spring a leak. You may not notice it at first. When the Titanic began to take on water, the passengers continued to sing and dance as if all was okay. We know how that turned out.

RULE #60

Relapse is not inevitable.

"While relapse rates in recovery are high, it is not inevitable that every recovering addict will experience a relapse."
Rudolph C. Hatfield

Statistics on relapse are all over the map. I would cite them here, but the numbers vary too widely from study to study. And the numbers don't really matter. What matters is what you will do about your own addiction.

When I introduce guys to my 90-Day Recovery Program, a common question is, "What is your success rate?" My answer is, "My success rate has been 100 percent since I got sober in January, 2015. But that's not the right question. The right question is, what will be your success rate? And that is completely up to you."

The best recovery program is the one you work. Relapse isn't some random curse thrust upon addicts against their will. Are you into tattoos? If so, you might want to get this stamped on your body someplace, the next time you decide that ink is the missing ingredient from the appearance you strive for.

"I'm as sober as I want to be."

No one ever put a gun to your head and made you act out against your will. You took your last drink because you wanted to. You had the affair because you wanted to. You popped the pills because you wanted to. You ordered the triple cheeseburger with bacon because you wanted to.

Relapse is a choice, and therefore is not inevitable.

I know it's hard to stay sober. That's why you need to pack your toolbox with every tool you can find – meetings, sessions, phone numbers, books, Scripture, prayer, church, exercise, healthy eating, good sleep, podcasts, sponsors, sponsees, conferences, meditation, journaling, recovery days, walks, worship music, and more.

But at the end of the day, there will be times when the answer simply has to be "No." Your past explains your addiction, but it doesn't excuse it. The next time you act out, it will be for one reason – you chose to. You can also choose not to. *Relapse is not inevitable.*

RULE #61

Recovery is a team sport.

*"A vision becomes a nightmare
when the leader has a big dream and a bad team."*
John Maxwell

I'll say it again. You can't maintain sobriety on your own. And even if you could, why would you want to? Never forget, the opposite of addiction is connection. Remember the Man Code. You need your 1, 3, 12, 120, and 5,000. When God created man, he said it was not good for him to be alone. You need others.

And others need you. If you have recovery figured out, please don't keep it to yourself! There are people all around you who need what you've got!

We all need a good recovery team. This team may include a sponsor, support group, 12-Step members, and others who share your common goal for sobriety. But not just anyone should have a place on your team. Here are a few things to look for in deciding who will be in your inner circle, or on your recovery team.

- Common goals. You all need to define sobriety the same way. You need to be striving for the same thing.
- Chemistry. You need a natural connection with the people on your team. This can't be forced. If you don't have this connection, they are not a good fit.

- Varied areas of expertise. You need people with long-term sobriety. You need others who have similar struggles to your own. You need people who are new to recovery. You need people with professional training on your team.
- Right foundation. I suggest that most of your team needs to share your values and spiritual convictions. For the most part, they should be Christ-followers.
- Willingness to kick people out. One of the hard things I've learned to do with my groups is to remove people who become toxic. Not everyone is a good fit. And just because they are a good fit today, that doesn't mean they will always be a good fit.

Yes, you need a team. They will be there for you, not because you're doing well, but because you're not. They will support you, encourage you, and correct you, when necessary. Choose this team wisely. The biggest difference in your recovery from now until this time next year will be the books you read and the people you spend time with.

RULE #62

Don't pray for motivation; pray for discipline.

"Discipline is the bridge between goals and achievement."
Jim Rohn

If we were only sober on the days when it was easy, nobody would be sober. If we only went to recovery meetings when we felt like it, attendance would be low. It's what we do when we don't want to do it that counts.

Think about your diet and exercise. There are times when you eat healthy, but your cravings for what's unhealthy drive you nuts. And there are times you spend on the treadmill that you would rather be anyplace else in the world. But regardless of motive and attitude, you still reap the same benefits.

There's an old saying in 12-Step groups: "Just bring the body." If we keep showing up, doing the right things, positive results will follow. We all want motivation. We pray for motivation. We wait for motivation. When we feel like staying sober, we will. If that's you, you are praying for the wrong thing. Don't pray for motivation. Pray for discipline.

Dr. Marty Nemko is a personal coach and author of ten books. He offers four principles in developing discipline that you might find helpful.

First, get comfortable being uncomfortable. It's okay to not enjoy therapy sessions, recovery groups, and daily recovery work.

No one said it would be easy. Or if they did, they were messing with you! Recovery work is not comfortable, especially at first.

Second, start short, simple, and easy. I discourage men who are in my 90-Day Program from working the 12 Steps at the same time. You need to do a few things well, rather than a bunch of things poorly. Start small, and go for easy wins.

Third, implement the Pomodoro Technique. It's simple. This technique requires you to work for 25 minutes, then play for five minutes. Make hobbies and other fun experiences a part of your recovery program.

Fourth, forgive yourself. Recovery is never linear. You will have setbacks (not necessarily relapses). Strive for progress over perfection. Give yourself room to be imperfect. No one works a perfect recovery program.

RULE #63

Jesus paid it all.

"Child of weakness, watch and pray. Find in me your all in all."
Jesus Paid It All, by Elvina Hall, 1878

Guilt and shame are two very different things. Guilt can be the tool of the Holy Spirit, correcting us when we do something wrong. God uses guilt to bring us to repentance and restoration. But shame is the tool of the enemy. While guilt says, "You've done something bad," shame screams, "You're a bad person." Shame will define you by your worst day. It will make you spiral downward.

About 150 years ago, Elvina Hall wrote a hymn that serves as the antidote to shame. My favorite verse is the last verse:

"And when, before the throne,
I stand in Him complete,
Jesus died my soul to save,
My lips shall still repeat."

When Jesus paid it all, he paid for the sins of your addiction. He paid for all the bad choices, your worst behaviors, and all of your slips and relapses. He paid for your guilt and washed away your shame. He paid for the wounds you caused others and he paid for a new life that you can choose to live or reject. Jesus paid it all.

Jonathan Parness serves as senior pastor for Cities Church in St. Paul, Minnesota. In reference to this timeless hymn, he writes, "We should beware of distancing ourselves from these words, of assuming that we are far removed from their relevance."

Jesus paid it all. That means you can smile. That means you can receive the peace that passes all understanding. That means you can relax. That means you win. Yes, Jesus paid it all. Not enough to get you a little sobriety, but all. Not enough to give you a little recovery, but all. Not enough to cover most of your past, but all. Jesus paid it all. Let that soak in for a few minutes.

RULE #64

Giving up on your recovery because of one setback is like slashing your other three tires because you had a flat.

"Setbacks motivate me."
Lindsey Vonn

An academic study was conducted in 2022 on what is known as the "setback effect." The issue addressed was the effect a setback has on us. The study came to three conclusions.

1. People are often not fully aware of the causes of setbacks. They tend to attribute a failure to internal causes while ignoring external ones.
2. Attributing setbacks to stable, internal factors beyond one's control can make future failures more likely. This is the definition of the setback effect.
3. A mindset shift to focus on external causes of a failure can prevent the setback effect.

The setback effect commonly occurs when a person attributes a failure to anything beyond his control. For example, when an addict blames his behaviors on his past, his genetics, or anything else beyond his control, he gives in to the addiction.

But when the addict attributes his behavior to something external, future setbacks are more easily avoided. These external forces are within his control – where he goes, who he sees, people he can avoid.

Everyone I know has had a flat tire. The answer is not to let the air out of the other three tires, but to fix the one that went flat. Treat your setbacks, slips, and relapses the same way. Don't quit just because you had a flat tire. The car is still good. You just need to take care of the flat.

Perhaps it will help to consider the setback effect. When you struggle, own it. Don't blame anyone but yourself. The good news is that you are the only person you control. By owning the setback, you can address that setback. You can fix the flat, get back on the road, and keep going.

RULE #65

Love yourself enough to set boundaries.

"Those who get angry when you set a boundary are the ones you need to set boundaries for."
J.S. Wolfe

We all know we need to set boundaries. The world is full of them. That's why you see "No Trespassing" signs. That's why you lock the doors of your house. And that's why you can't just show up at the doctor's office without an appointment. Boundaries are a part of life.

Let's consider the difference between boundaries that are healthy and those that are not. A healthy boundary protects you from getting taken advantage of; an unhealthy boundary allows you to be used. With good boundaries, you own your time; with poor boundaries, others own your time. Healthy boundaries allow you to spend time for yourself; unhealthy boundaries let others walk all over you. With healthy boundaries, you can say no; with unhealthy boundaries, you seldom say no. And healthy boundaries allow you to set limits on others without feeling bad; unhealthy boundaries make you feel guilty when you set limits on others.

Now let's get practical. There are five ways to set good boundaries.

1. Identify your limits. They cannot be abstract. Be as specific as possible. Produce a daily agenda, with time carved out for what matters most, so you don't get off track with distractions.
2. Communicate your boundaries. Let those close to you know your limits. Give them your schedule. Brene Brown says it like this: "Clear is kind, unclear is unkind."
3. Stick to your boundaries. They need to be in ink, not pencil. If you let your boundaries shift around, you might as well ditch them.
4. Learn to say no. This is nearly impossible for some people, including me. But "No" is a complete sentence. Follow it with a period, not a comma.
5. Make time for yourself. If you are no good to yourself, you will be of no good to others. This needs to be a daily thing. And time for yourself should take priority.

Boundaries. If you are to stay sober, you must first be healthy. And without boundaries, you will never be healthy. So set boundaries. That will make you a better person. Your recovery will thank you for that.

RULE #66

You'll never know you're sober until you're tested.

"To be tested is good.
The challenged life may be the best therapist."
Gail Sheehy

In school, I always loved test days – if I was prepared. I wasn't too crazy about pop quizzes. Life is full of pop quizzes. Sometimes, you know when you'll be tested, but not usually. Recovery works the same way. There are plenty of times when you know you will be tested – parties, trips to the beach, dinner with your in-laws. But there are unpredictable pop quizzes nearly every day. You're watching a television program with your spouse, and a sexual scene comes out of nowhere. You are at a company outing when someone offers you a drink. You are on family vacation, and routine is hard to come by.

Basketball legend Jerry West said, "I've seen a lot in my life. I've seen a lot of winning, and I've seen a lot of testing times. I think when you're tested, you really find out what you're made of."

The key to passing any test is preparation. There are several things you can do to be ready when the next test comes your way.

First, develop new coping strategies. Before the temptation hits, plan your response. How will you cope when tempted to take a drink? Or when you see an attractive person enter the room? Or when you want more pain medicine than you should take?

Second, be okay with struggles. It's okay to be tempted. It's okay to feel anxious. This is part of life. Know that there will be days like that, days when life is not as easy. Be okay with that.

Third, build new relationships. You can't get through this on your own. You need others. Remember, recovery is a team sport. Find new friends on whom you can rely.

Fourth, watch out for boredom. This is one of the five basic triggers. When bored, your mind can easily stray. So keep your mind busy. And when necessary, change your place and change your pace.

Fifth, remember the end game. If you give in to the temptation, you know how this will end. You have felt the guilt. You have sat in the shame. It's not worth it.

RULE #67

Your sobriety is only as strong as your next decision.

"It is in your moments of decision that your destiny is shaped."
Tony Robbins

Billy Graham said, "The difference between one person and another is the decisions they make." In my life, that has really been true. I can trace my greatest blessings to the decisions I made. I chose Jesus as my Savior. We chose to have a child. I chose the right college and seminary. I chose the right churches to pastor and the right places to live. And Beth and I chose the right ministry when we launched There's Still Hope. And we chose the right name for this ministry.

I've made some bad decisions, as well. I chose to live in my addiction in secret for three decades. I chose to act out each time; no one made me do that. I chose to waste time and treasure on things that never satisfy. I've made a lot of bad decisions, and I paid for each one of them.

Robert Schuller said, "Never cut a tree down in the wintertime. Never make a negative decision in the low time. Never make your most important decisions when you are in your worst moods. Wait. Be patient. The storm will pass. The spring will come."

Timing is everything.

The best way to make good decisions is to have a good process for how you make decisions. Let's consider a few ways to put yourself in the best position to make good decisions.

1. Seek the counsel of others. Remember the two great questions in life? What is the wise thing to do? What do you think is the wise thing to do? Seek the advice of others.
2. Address the cause, not just the symptoms. Otherwise, you'll be right back with the same dilemma tomorrow. Dig deep, and you'll be able to climb high.
3. Be accountable. The reason many addicts make bad decisions is that they have no accountability in place. Every bad decision should come with consequences.
4. Look at the big picture. Addicts are myopic people. We are near-sighted. We only see the immediate pleasure. We need to consider the ramifications.
5. Put what you want most ahead of what you want now. Think long game. Ask yourself, "What will tomorrow wish I had done today?"

You get to pick your decisions, but not your consequences. So make them wisely. What you do today will change tomorrow. You can make whatever decisions you want, but remember, after you make your decisions, your decisions will make you.

RULE #68

If you get well for anyone but yourself, it won't last.

"Love your neighbor as you love yourself."
Jesus

The second command, Jesus said, was to love others as you love yourself. Not *before* you love yourself, but *as* you love yourself.

It is common for a man or woman caught in an addiction to proclaim to those closest to him or her, "I will never do this to you again!" And it's true. Not hurting our loved ones is a good motivation to stay sober. But it's not a *great* motivation to stay sober. I have known hundreds, if not thousands of addicts. Not one of them ever got sober for someone else, *and stayed sober*.

Let me get personal. Friend, the person you hurt more than anyone else with your addiction was not your husband or wife, son or daughter. It was YOU! You hurt yourself. Your intent to protect those around you from your addiction is commendable. But it won't work. That is, unless you get sober for yourself, first, and then for the sake of others.

When my addiction was uncovered, I didn't know if my marriage would last. My therapist told me that my marriage was secondary to my recovery. That sounded crazy at the time. But the fact is that if you, as an addict, try to save your marriage by staying sober, you will probably lose your marriage and your sobriety. But if you get sober first, you have a good chance of maintaining both your recovery and your marriage.

I repeat – if you get well for anyone but yourself, it won't last. Here are a few tips to get you started:

- Get in a recovery group right away. Go into it with eyes wide open. There is no perfect group. But there is an old saying from AA that goes like this: "The measure we gave was the measure we got back."
- Make amends to yourself. Skip on to Step 9. "We made amends to those we had harmed, unless to do so would injure them or others." You don't need to make amends to the whole world right away, just to yourself.
- Chart a new course. Plan a program, with the help of your therapist or sponsor. Your plan should include meetings, recovery work, spiritual disciplines, physical self-care, and hobbies. Yes, I said hobbies.
- Reward success. Do something good for yourself to mark milestones in your recovery, beginning with 24 hours. Then one week, and one month. Turn this into a monthly Recovery Day.

RULE #69

You're as sober as you want to be.

"Destiny is not a matter of chance. It is a matter of choice."
William Jennings Bryan

Rob wrote a list, and he checked it twice. This time, he was going to kill it:

- Make a healthy snack.
- Go to the gym.
- Don't waste time on social media.
- Read a classic novel.
- Housetrain Fido.

A mere 24 hours later, Rob sat munching on celery sticks as he read *The Great Gatsby*. His legs were sore, but in a good way. After an hour on the treadmill, he saw Fido waiting patiently at the back door, so he could go out and do his business.

Now, for the real news. Rob was on his couch, one hand in a bag of chips, and the other on his cell phone. His unopened gym bag sat on the kitchen table next to his *Archie* comic book. And, of course, there was a fresh spot on the carpet.

We don't change overnight. But we can change. Rob was doing exactly what he wanted to do. He said he wanted to establish better habits; his intentions are commendable. Actually, they aren't. Because intentions without follow-through mean nothing.

At the end of the day, you are exactly as sober as you want to be. If you *really* wanted to quit your habit, you would. My mom wanted to quit smoking for 60 years. But she didn't quit until she *really* wanted to stop. You are no different. If you were serious about recovery, you would find a therapist, get to a group every day, work a program, complete the Steps, pray more, read Scripture more, and practice healthy self-care.

Here's the #1 reason you act out. Ready for this? *You want to.* You will never get sober until you turn what you *ought* to do into what you *want* to do. And only you can measure your desire. But Jesus was right. We are known by our fruit. So if you really want to be sober, those around you will see a change. You become what you really want to be.

RULE #70

The key to recovery is found in your daily agenda.

"It all comes down to what you do daily."
John Maxwell

You find recovery the same way you found addiction – by doing the same thing over and over each day. You need a daily agenda. Otherwise, you are just hoping to stay sober. But hope is not a plan. Here are some principles you need to understand:

- You will never change your life until you change the things you do daily.
- You are always preparing for something.
- The most important hour of the day isn't what you think.

Let me explain that last one. The most important hour of the day, according to *Entrepreneur*, comes in two parts – 30 minutes in the morning and 30 minutes before bed. In those first 30 minutes, you need to review your day, adjust plans as needed, pray, and prepare for the day. During the last 30 minutes, you need to reflect on your day and review the day to come.

As for your daily agenda, here are some good suggestions from Craig Simpson, an Oregon-based entrepreneur and author.

- Start the day right.
- Have a plan for what you want to accomplish.
- Break tasks into reasonable units.
- Prioritize what matters and forget the rest.
- Delegate when possible.
- Plan time for meals, exercise, and socializing.
- Follow each big push with relaxation.
- End each day with a plan for tomorrow.

Now, apply this to recovery. Create an agenda for your daily recovery work. Yes, I said *daily* recovery work. Addiction never takes a day off; neither should recovery. So plan your day carefully. Include prayer, reading, meditation, reflection, calls, meetings, exercise – anything that keeps you in a good place. You don't need to do a lot any day, but you do need to do something every day.

RULE #71

Do something today that your future will thank you for.

"Destiny is not a matter of chance, but of choice."
William Jennings Bryan

The level of your sobriety tomorrow will be the predictable result of the things you do today. Each year, on my sobriety date, I take a new chip marking that milestone. But the most significant part of that day is not receiving the chip; it is the work I do to stay sober for the next 24 hours.

One of the best gifts you can give yourself is to do recovery work today that tomorrow will thank you for. Here are a few ways to do that.

First, aim for growth. There are two kinds of people – those who see their gifts as set in stone and innate, and those who see their gifts as something to be developed. The second group does better in recovery, because they own their future, rather than react to it. Never stop learning and never stop growing in your recovery.

Second, remain curious. Walt Disney said, "We keep moving forward, opening new doors, and doing new things, because we're curious, and curiosity keeps leading us down new paths." Remain curious about recovery. When you attend meetings, bring your questions and leave your answers at the door.

Third, create a clear vision. Define your three circles. Know what sobriety looks like for you. Set specific goals. Mike Murdock was right: "The secret of your future is hidden in your daily routine." Establish that routine. "The best way to predict your future is to create it" (Joe Dispenza). So do that. Create a clear picture of what you want your recovery to look like.

Fourth, adjust as needed. You need dreams. You need hope. We all do. But what you really need is a plan. And that plan must be flexible. William Shakespeare wrote, "Suit the action to the word, the word to the action." One way to assure that you'll have a better future is to quit trying to have a better past. Own the past, then move on from it. Create a recovery plan for the future, but be willing to adjust as needed.

RULE #72

You have nothing to fear when you have nothing to hide.

"With integrity, you have nothing to fear,
since you have nothing to hide."
Zig Ziglar

Beth Ann Helgason and Jonathan Lev Berman conducted an interesting study for the London Business School. They worked with a large group of volunteers, who were put into three categories. The prerequisite to being a part of the project was that the volunteers have things they had done which they had not shared with anyone, but knew they should. Group A was told to fully disclose their behaviors to the appropriate person. For example, if they had been unfaithful to their spouse, they would confess everything to their spouse.

Group B was told to withhold their information for the duration of the project. And Group C agreed to do a partial disclosure of their inappropriate actions. Then, after a period of time, the three groups were brought back together and given a series of questions to answer. The researchers were seeking to discover which of the three groups felt better about themselves following the process.

Not surprisingly, Group A felt the most positive. By getting it all out, they felt better about themselves, their own integrity, and their future. Their sleep habits had improved, as had their personal relationships. But this is where things got interesting.

The group that felt the worst was Group C. The group that completely withheld all information actually felt better about themselves than the group that told half-truths. The researchers concluded from the data that this was because Group C felt conflicted. Having to remember what they had said and not said tormented them. It was impossible for them to move on. They were the most anxious of the three groups.

Telling our secrets is far less painful than withholding them. And I'm not talking about what it does to your loved ones; I'm talking about what it does to you. A partial disclosure is worse than no disclosure at all. But what trumps it all is to release everything. Get it all out. Once you have nothing to hide, you have nothing to fear. And that is where freedom begins.

RULE #73

Addiction takes you further than you want to go, keeps you longer than you want to stay, and costs you more than you want to pay.

"Grace is the gift of God to not sin."
John Piper

Addiction will take you just as you are, but it never leaves you that way. Its effects are profound and lasting. That's why no one ever looks back on their addictive behaviors and says, "That was a good idea."

A recent article in *National Geographic* considered the effects of addiction. The author, Fran Smith, concluded, "Addiction remolds neural circuits to assign supreme value to cocaine or heroin or gin at the expense of other interests such as health, work, family, or life itself." His study found that addiction causes hundreds of changes to the chemistry of the brain. It remaps the brain and causes it to focus only on one thing – the object of its desire. All else is blotted out.

That is a perfect description of what happens when we are caught up in our addiction. Nothing else matters; we crave the next "hit" with reckless abandon. Smith summarizes his findings: "The brain changes your ability to put the lid on desire."

Elliott Redwine takes this even further, with research on the effects of addiction beyond the damage it does to the addict.

Among his findings is that one in eight children lives with a parent who has an active substance abuse problem. The effects become generational.

Here are just a few of the impacts of addiction:

- Damages the spiritual connection between the addict and God
- Injures those closest to the addict
- Steals time and money
- Progresses to other addictions
- Takes away self-esteem and self-confidence
- Threatens the addict's health
- Harms the capacity for rational thought

It would be impossible to overstate the effects of addiction. Let's end where we began. Addiction will take you further than you want to go, keep you longer than you want to stay, and cost you more than you want to pay.

RULE #74

Every shortcut is a dead end.

"There are no shortcuts to any place worth going."
Beverly Sills

We live in the microwave era. We love fast food and fast cars. We want everything to come quickly and easily. Recently, Major League Baseball made rule changes for one reason – to get the game over faster. We are impatient. We tape *60 Minutes* so we can watch it in 45 minutes.

Some things are okay that way. But recovery isn't one of them. In recovery, every shortcut is a dead end. I had a sponsee ask me, "How long will it take me to complete the 12 Steps?" I said, "It all depends on how hard you are willing to work at it. If you do a *good* job, it can be done in six months. If you do a *great* job, it will take you a year."

There are several reasons recovery is better *because* there are no shortcuts.

1. Experience takes time. The only way to get your one-month chip in less than 30 days is to do it in February. Solid recovery is the compilation of a lot of good experiences. And they can't be rushed.
2. Feedback makes you stronger. By slowing things down, you can involve more people. You can get the feedback

from a sponsor, therapist, and others in your group. The more feedback you get, the better off you will be.

3. It takes time to create solutions. There will be a lot of trial and error. You may need to switch sponsors at some point. (I certainly did.) You will need to try different groups, complete certain programs, and read certain books. There are no shortcuts for that.

4. You need time to build relationships. The biggest difference in your recovery one year from now will be in the relationships you build. As I look back over my years of sobriety, I can trace it all to the people I have met and invested in.

Shortcuts might get you to the finish line quicker, but when you get there, you will realize you have yet to arrive. The work isn't done. You will still have Steps to review, lessons to learn, and books to read. Shortcuts deny us the opportunity that the journey provides.

Have you ever driven the Blue Ridge Parkway? There are a lot faster ways to get from Georgia to Pennsylvania. But why would you want to take the Interstate and miss all the great views? Recovery cannot be rushed. Every shortcut is really a dead end.

RULE #75

The pain of discipline is less than the pain of regret.

"Discipline weighs ounces, while regret weighs tons."
Jim Rohn

I live a pretty disciplined life. But it's not easy. I have to discipline myself to be disciplined. But if I don't do that, I live in regrets. I have to pick one or the other – discipline or regret. Let me give you an example from my high school years.

When I was 13, Dad said, "Here you go!" And he presented me with a tenor saxophone. "We need a woodwind in the family," he explained. "I play trombone, your brother plays trumpet, and Mom plays piano." So it was the sax for me. But I loved it! It didn't take long for me to discover the tenor sax is the most desired instrument in any jazz band. It produces a sound like no other.

The problem was that Dad hedged his bet. He hoped I'd really enjoy the sax, but he wasn't sure. So he bought me a King Cleveland model, not a great instrument. I did my research. "Dad, I want a Selmer Mark VI," I said. The Selmer Mark VI was the finest tenor sax ever built. (It still is.) Dad made me a deal. "When you make first chair in the high school band, I'll buy you a Selmer Mark VI." So I took lessons. I practiced several hours a day. And sure enough, in my first year in high school, I made first chair.

I was first chair in marching band, concert band, symphonic band, and jazz band. I was really good. Not great, but really good. But then I stopped getting better, since I had my Selmer Mark VI and was first chair. I quit practicing at home. I was good enough to keep first chair without practice. But I stagnated. Even though I went on to play in my college band, I was a better sax player at age 15 than I was in college.

I lacked discipline. Now I look back at what could have been, and I have regrets.

Recovery is like that. You can live a life of discipline – work the Steps, sponsor others, pray every morning, read recovery material every day, go to meetings every week. Or you can coast. Don't put in the hard work; do just enough to get by and stay out of your inner circle. But if you do that, one day you will look back with a heart filled with regret.

Remember, discipline weighs ounces, while regret weighs a ton.

RULE #76

You can't lust without falling any more than you can jump off a building without hitting the ground.

"Lust's passion will be served; it demands,
it militates, it tyrannizes."
Marquis de Sade

Rob Weiss wrote a fascinating book, *Out of the Doghouse: A Step-by-Step Relationship-Saving Guide for Men Caught Cheating*. In the book, he talks about the effects of lust. "People who utilize sexual desire and fantasy as a primary coping mechanism can lose touch with the real world and the actual people in it. They can lose their ability to connect and be intimate."

That is what lust does for you. Any recovering sex addict knows that the definition of recovery is not the absence of acting out, but progressive victory over lust. We think actions have consequences, and they do. But thoughts have consequences, also. What you think today, you will do tomorrow. It is inevitable. The addiction cycle has never changed:

1. I think it.
2. I plan it.
3. I do it.
4. I hate it.

5. I cover it.
6. I do it again.

There are two serious problems with any relationship that is based on lust, according to Dawson McAllister. First, such a relationship is rooted in self-indulgence. We are using the other person rather than blessing the other person. Love can hardly wait to give; lust can hardly wait to get. Lust drives us into the ditch every time.

The other problem with lust in a relationship is that the person filled with lust abandons the other person when he is no longer getting what he wants. McAllister writes, "I can't tell you how many times girls have called me on my show to announce they were pregnant, their boyfriend is long gone, and they are left all alone."

It would be crazy to climb to the top of a building and announce, "Okay, watch this! I'm going to jump off, but I won't hit the ground when I fall." It would be just as insane to say to yourself, "I will indulge in a little lust. No one will get hurt."

RULE #77

Your present is not your future.

"We don't wait for a better future. We create it."
Marty Walsh

It feels like whatever is going on will never end. This is especially true for couples who have been rocked by addiction. We hear it all the time. "My wife will never get sober." "My husband will never be faithful." "They will never change." "I can't get over this addiction."

When you are sober for 30 days, you feel like you'll never act out again. And when you relapse, you feel like you'll never be sober again. But here's the deal – your present is not your future. Wherever you are in your recovery today, I promise you, in a year, you will be in a different place. Will it be a better place? That's up to you.

Mark Cuban knows a little bit about growing a business. He said, "Leaders don't look backwards to condemn what has already been done; they look forward to create a better future."

There are several ways to create that better future, for your life and for your recovery.

- Find your niche. Figure out what works for you. What keeps your buddy sober may not be as valuable to you. For some, it's about going to meetings every day. Others love to journal. Some make multiple calls each day. You need to do what works for you. A successful recovery program is tailor-made for the person in that program.

- Adjust your attitude. Whether you think you can stay sober or you think you can't stay sober, you are probably right. Attitude is everything. People who live in the past and spend all their time on their mistakes stay there. You need to look forward. Lift your head and look in the mirror and repeat positive affirmations. Start with this one – if God is for you, no one can come against you!

- Take care of yourself physically. Too many addicts keep swapping out one addiction for another. They tend to drink too much, eat too much, and exercise too little. Your physical being is connected to your spiritual, emotional, and mental being. So take care of yourself physically. Start with good exercise and rest.

- Make a plan. The future is coming, whether you're ready for it or not. If you hope to grow in your sobriety, you need to plan for it. No one ever stumbled into recovery. No one outgrows addiction. Long-term sobriety is the result of a concentrated program that results from careful and prayerful planning.

RULE #78

One is too many, and 1,000 is not enough.

"I can't get no satisfaction."
The Rolling Stones

If what you already have doesn't satisfy, why would more of it make things better? But that's how we think. John Rockefeller was asked how much money it takes to be happy. He said, "A little bit more." Jay Leno was asked why he had 300 classic cars. He said, "Because 299 wasn't enough."

Tal Ben-Shahar, co-founder of the online Happiness Studies Academy, conducted an interesting study on people who have significant, sudden gains in their lives. He concluded, "Most people believe that if you win the lottery or get that raise or promotion, or win a tournament, then you'll be all set. This actually leads millions of people on the path to unhappiness. Because at best, what success does is lead to a temporary spike in our levels of wellbeing, not to lasting happiness."

Research suggests that Americans' happiness peaks at $75,000 per year. Once they reach that level of income, where there needs can be met, their happiness hits its highest level. Any additional money beyond that has no effect of additional happiness.

The Baylor Bears had not won a Southwest Conference Championship since 1924, and they had not beaten the University of Texas since 1956. And then it happened, on November 9, 1974. Trailing Texas at the half, 24-7, Baylor mounted a comeback that would be known as the "Miracle on the Brazos." Quarterback Neal Jeffrey led his team to a 34-24 victory and the conference championship. It was the high water mark of his career – college and pro. Late that night, still savoring the victory, Jeffrey returned to the stadium to look at the scoreboard, still lit up: Baylor 34, Texas 24. And then he said to himself, "Is that all there is?"

Addiction works the same way. One is too many, because it only leads to more. But 1,000 isn't enough, because it never satisfies. Money, careers, achievements, and addictions – they never satisfy. Dallin H. Oaks explains, "You can never get enough of what you don't need, because what you don't need won't satisfy you."

RULE #79

Remorse is great, but repentance is better.

"Of all acts of man repentance is the most divine."
Thomas Carlyle

Every addict I know has remorse for what he has done. The ones who don't have remorse never show up to recovery meetings. When someone reaches out to our ministry for help, remorse is inevitable. I was the same way. My remorse was heavy. There were endless tears accompanied with a broken heart for the carnage I had caused. And that's a great start. But sadly, it's just not enough.

Remorse says, "I feel awful for what I've done." But it doesn't chart a new course. That's where repentance comes in. In remorse, we regret what we have done. But in repentance we do something about it. Billy Graham said, "The wonderful news is that our Lord is a God of mercy, and he responds to repentance." Jesus said that he had come "to call sinners to repentance," not remorse.

Jeff Bedwell, pastor of the First Baptist Church of Fort Mill, South Carolina, preached a great message on this in 2021. He said, "There is a difference between remorse and repentance. Remorse is primarily sorrowful for the consequences of our sins. Repentance is primarily sorrowful for sinning against the love and holiness of God."

What about you? Do you have remorse or repentance? Has your addiction brought great sorrow, embarrassment, and shame? Has it taken you further than that? Repentance is a change of mind that results in a change of direction. If you have not changed your behavior, you may have deep sorrow and remorse. But you haven't yet repented.

If this prayer represents the conviction of your heart, make it yours today.

"Dear God, I fully own my addictive behaviors. I have failed to address my addiction as fully as I should have, and for that I have deep regrets. But I want to go beyond that. I commit to a lifestyle of repentance. I will change directions. From this day forward, I will live a different life, marked by different habits. I will do whatever it takes to stay sober and to be a person of integrity."

RULE #80

Recovery is giving up what you want now for what you want most.

"Successful people keep moving.
They make mistakes, but they don't quit."
Conrad Hilton

Every time you smoke the cigarette, drink the gin, bet on your team, view pornography, or indulge in some other addiction, you do it for one simple reason. It's not that complicated. Sure, you would do well to do the hard work of therapy. Look at your family history. Dig into past trauma. Ask why you are triggered by the things that trigger you. But at the end of the day, every time you act out it is because . . .

You choose what you want now over what you want most.

What you want most is sobriety. You want recovery. You want serenity. You want integrity. You want honesty. You want all of these things, and 99 percent of the time, it's obvious, because 99 percent of the time, you pursue those things. But cancer in one percent of your body can be deadly. And acting out one percent of the time can ruin everything.

Do the math. If you were sober 99 percent of the time, you'd be acting out for 15 minutes every day. That's enough time to drink several beers, place a bet, eat a box of donuts, and call an old girlfriend. You can break your sobriety in a lot less time than

15 minutes. And that's every day. Obviously, you want to do better than that.

So you need to be on your game every day, all the time. And you need to recognize your selfish nature. When you give in to your urges, call it what it is. Say this, "I am choosing what I want now over what I want most." At least be honest about it.

How can you keep what you want most in the forefront of your thinking? Try a few things:

- Pray the 7th Step Prayer every morning.
- Remember the end game, every time you think about breaking your sobriety.
- Keep a family photo on your desk.
- Keep healthy guardrails in place.
- Stay as far from those guardrails as possible.
- Remember what it felt like the last time you acted out.
- Call someone every time you get close to the line.

RULE #81

Two years is huge.

"Milestones aren't what I think about much."
Craig Newmark

A common question is, "How much sobriety do I need to get over the hump?" It's a good question. I have read dozens of studies on the subject. Some research indicates that until people have 18 months of sobriety, relapse still runs above 50 percent, and that after 18 months, the number is less than 50 percent. Other studies put that number at two years of sobriety, or a bit longer. If you average out all the studies (I'm a math geek), you come to this conclusion.

On balance, once a person gets to two years of sobriety, he is more likely than not to stay sober for the rest of his life.

That doesn't mean you're in the clear after two years, nor does it mean you are doomed to fail if you've only been sober for two hours. Every two years starts with two hours! But it is interesting. While we could spend hours trying to answer the question, "Why two years?" I think it would be more helpful to hear from someone who has two years of sobriety.

I don't know Alicia Gilbert, but I find her story to be compelling. From two years of sobriety from alcohol, she identifies six things she has learned.

1. Alcohol isn't the real problem. Gilbert says that in order for a person to stay sober, she needs to answer these questions: Why do I drink excessively? What feelings am I trying to escape? As I often say, addiction isn't a bad problem; it's a bad solution.
2. Get a therapist. The problem for most addicts, Gilbert suggests, is that they think their addiction gives them immense, intuitive knowledge as to *why* they are addicts. But this is where professional counsel is beneficial.
3. Sugar cravings are natural. In other words, when you stop one addiction, prepare to find another one. It is common for new urges to pop up in place of old ones that we are no longer feeding.
4. Not everyone will forgive and be your friend, and that's okay. It is important to let people go. You will be surprised by those who stick with you and by many who won't.
5. You'll never feel completely good about your past, so don't try. At some point, it is unhealthy to keep trying to find every reason for every behavior. Work the 9th Step and make amends. Then move on.
6. If you want to help yourself, help others. It is never too early to work the 12th Step. This gets your eyes off your own problems and provides a great sense of worth. Find someone with less than two years sobriety and be their friend.

RULE #82

Freedom is a choice more than a condition.

"Nothing is more difficult, and therefore more precious, than to be able to decide."
Napoleon

"I am free of my addiction!" my friend exclaimed. The next week, he relapsed. So what gives? If he was free, why did he relapse? Did God let him down? I mean, if we are free, we're free, right? Well, sort of. Here's the inconvenient truth.

Freedom is a choice more than it is a condition.

I have a friend who has been free for 30 years. I have another buddy whose sobriety date goes back 22 years. And I know a man who has been free for 24 hours. So who is really free? They all are. You see, freedom is a choice. It is available to all of us. God doesn't mystically choose some of us to be free, while leaving the others in bondage. That's not the kind of God we serve.

God's desire is that all would be free. And he has provided the same avenue to freedom for every addict. He is no respecter of persons. God doesn't say, "Let's see, Larry over there is in a really cool church. They lay hands on people and pray for them. I'll make Larry free. But Jim goes to a different kind of church. He doesn't worship the same way. I believe I'll leave him in bondage."

God offers freedom to every one of us. Think of it like his offer of salvation. While it is a gift, that gift must be received. God doesn't force his grace on anyone. The hymn says it well: "I have decided to follow Jesus." Call it free will. Call it what you want, but it's how God works. He wants us all to be free. And if we work our program and want it badly enough, here's the good news:

We will be free.

I am not free today because I had a supernatural encounter with God several years ago. I'm free today, because I met with him yesterday. And this morning. I'm free today because I choose to be. As of this writing, I have made that same choice every day for 3,102 days in a row. And I like it this way.

Think of how bad it would be if you got "free" several year ago, and that was it. No more addiction. Problem solved. Case closed. What would that do for your desperation meter? I mean, wouldn't you be just a tad less hungry for God's help and blessing in your life? Sure, you would. You can be free today, if you choose to be. So do it – choose to be.

RULE #83

Remember the end game.

"I've been truly blessed. I've taken my time, kept my eye on the prize, and done what I've had to do. So I'm able to make a choice when to retire. Most fighters really couldn't."
Floyd Mayweather, Jr.

It was some of the best advice my sponsor ever gave me. "Remember the end game." Here's the context. Early in my sobriety, I was in a situation that was quite triggering. So I called him for advice. He said, "Go ahead, think through what you are tempted to do. Think about how you would pull it off. But don't stop there. Think of the end game. Remind yourself how things end if you act out. It doesn't end well."

I've taught that principle many times. It is as effective a tool as I know. Our natural tendency is to only think about the immediate pleasure. But when we remember the end game, this serves as a terrific deterrent to what we are thinking. Here are some of the results that cross our minds when we remember the end game.

- Broken trust with our spouse
- Reset our sobriety date
- Overwhelming guilt
- Doubts of ever staying sober

- Damaged spiritual connection
- Deep sense of shame
- Blown personal testimony
- Having to tell my group
- Having to tell my sponsor
- Having to tell my sponsees

No one ever relapses and says, "I'm so glad I did!" I guarantee you the last thing the enemy wants you to do is to remember the end game. He is committed to keeping your eye on what is in front of you – the next image, drink, pill, etc. He knows the power of the end game. The last thing he wants is for you to think about the consequences of what you might do.

A recent study found that negative feelings are twice as powerful as positive ones. A large group of sports fans was monitored for their emotional feelings, based on the outcome of a game. The study group was split evenly, with half the people pulling for one team and the other half supporting the other team. Each person's emotions were monitored. The conclusion was that when a fan's team did poorly or lost the game, his emotional reaction was twice as strong as the emotions of the fans whose team did well.

Consequences are motivators. Remember the end game.

RULE #84

A lone sheep is a dead sheep.

"The way a team plays as a whole determines its success."
Babe Ruth

Matthew 18:12-13 *"If a man owns a hundred sheep, and one of them wanders away, will he not leave the 99 on the hills and go to look for the one that wandered off? And if he finds it, truly I tell you, he is happier about that one sheep than about the 99 that did not wander off."*

Jesus knew that a lone sheep is a dead sheep. In the Bible, sheep represent God's children. You are one of his sheep, and he is your Good Shepherd. What is true with sheep is true with us. We can't make it on our own, especially in recovery.

Over the years, I have observed as dozens of men have slowly slipped out of my 12-Step group. When I reach out to some of them, the news is almost never good. In a few cases, they have moved out of town or joined a new group. But in the vast majority of the cases, the man who no longer attends a group has relapsed and strayed light years from his recovery.

Which comes first, the chicken or the egg?

Does a person quit the group because he has had a relapse? Or does he relapse because he has quit the group?

Yes and yes. It can be either. And it can be both. But what I have found is that in most cases, the guy who quits the group is already in the early stages of relapse. But when he loses the contact and support of the group, he spirals quickly.

We are wired for human connection.

In 1933, British explorer Frank Smythe attempted to climb Mt. Everest alone. He became so convinced that someone else was with him on the climb that he offered a piece of cake to his invisible partner. And in 1895, Joshua Slocum became the first person to circumnavigate the globe in a sailboat singlehandedly. He said that in the most difficult moments the pilot of Christopher Columbus' ship *The Pinta* joined him aboard his vessel.

Isolation does crazy things to us. Whether you are climbing mountains, sailing around the world, or just trying to make it to the next day, never travel alone. You weren't created for that. Isolation is never your friend.

RULE #85

You get what you tolerate.

"Tolerance is the virtue of the man without convictions."
Gilbert Chesterton

It's true for the wounded spouse. If your husband or wife has betrayed you, that's on them. But if you don't put up boundaries, guardrails, and consequences, well, that's on you. What you call grace may really be enabling them to continue down their dangerous path, putting you both in peril. Don't misunderstand. Their actions are on them. It's not about you. The addict must own his behavior, 100 percent. But for the sake of your own health (mental, emotional, and physical), it is critical that you draw a line that cannot be crossed without consequences.

It's also true for the addict. You get what you tolerate. If you allow toxic people into your life, that's on you. If you allow certain movies into your home, that's on you. If you let a coworker continue to walk all over you, that's on you.

You get what you tolerate.

There are several principles at play in the arena of toleration. Let's talk about a few of them.

1. Toleration is not a sign of strength. People-pleasers really struggle here. They want to be liked, so they put up with all kinds of abuse. This comes from personal insecurities

that need to be addressed. Until you love yourself, no one else will.

2. Toleration always makes things worse. As we've said, when you tolerate another person's abuse, you are enabling them to practice more abuse. This not only hurts you, it delays their recovery.

3. What you allow to visit today will become your roommate tomorrow. If you accept a little abuse or a little acting out, this will become the new normal. Your tomorrow won't be happy with what you are doing today.

4. You can't compromise with addiction. Tolerating a little indulgence will set you up for a huge fall. If you are an alcoholic, you can't drink a little wine. If you are a video game addict, you can't play a single game. Well, you can, but you shouldn't.

Football legend Gale Sayers said, "There comes a time when you have to stand up and be counted." And my favorite theologian, LL Cool J, said, "Stand up and face your fears, or they will defeat you." Sayers and J (Is that his last name?) are both right. If you value your own sanity, if you put a premium on your own recovery, stand up for yourself. Be careful about what you tolerate, because that which you tolerate today will own you tomorrow.

RULE #86

The best way to defeat fantasies is to quit creating new ones.

"We live in a fantasy world, a world of illusion. The great task in life is to find reality."
Iris Murdoch

If you want to understand fantasy, I recommend Jay Stringer's groundbreaking book, *Unwanted*. But for our purposes, when we think of sexual addiction, we know that fantasy is not a good thing. Most men want what they shouldn't have, then don't want it once they have it. They fantasize about sexual experiences, as well as potential and past partners. And that leads to relapse. But it goes deeper than that.

Wendy Maltz has written extensively on the subject. She says, "If left untreated, sexual fantasies can cause many problems. They can lower self-esteem, lead to risky sexual behavior, cause sexual functioning problems, and harm intimacy with a partner." Fantasy does more damage than just putting images on one's mind that stay for years.

D.E. Nutter has studied the impact of fantasy on sexual performance. His research concludes, "The frequency of fantasy was greatest among men who developed erectile dysfunction." In layman's terms, when a man turns to fantasy, images, and pornography, "the real thing" suddenly becomes less fulfilling. He has created his own Twilight Zone. His wife is an occasional guest, but not the main star.

The good news is that old fantasies fade. The bad news is that this doesn't happen quickly. That's why you can remember the guy or girl you were attracted to in the 7th grade, but you don't remember the difference between a verb and a noun. Images you took in decades ago can still haunt you today. There are two answers.

1. Create new memories. Old memories need to be replaced with healthy memories of your spouse, kids, vacations, and other significant moments.
2. Quit taking in new images. The best way to overcome fantasies is to quit loading new ones into your brain. When you see an attractive person, look away. Avoid certain media, places, and people.

Fantasy can be a huge problem for anyone dealing with addiction. Fantasy will give you a "hit" when you want it, where you want it. But it's not real. And it only corrupts what is real. You can't do anything about the images you have already taken in. But you can do this – quit taking in new ones.

RULE #87

The real blessing is not the sobriety we seek, but the journey we walk.

"Joy is found not in finishing an activity, but in doing it."
Greg Anderson

If they handed out graduation diplomas for recovery, I'd skip the ceremony. I don't want to graduate, because the journey is too rich. Recovery is like a vacation. There are so many things to see on the way that sometimes, you don't even want to get to your destination. The magic is in the journey.

This took a long time for me to embrace. I'm a task-oriented, goal-obsessed person. I can't help myself. But I like what Michael Neil says in his book, *Supercoach*: "Obsessing about goals is like playing a game of fetch with yourself, using your happiness and self-worth as the bone." Tennis legend Arthur Ashe said, "Success is a journey, not a destination. The doing is often more important than the outcome."

What makes this journey so sweet? Several things:

- The connections you make
- The resources you gather
- The Steps you work
- The meetings you attend
- The prayers you pray

- The Scriptures you learn
- The people you sponsor
- The habits you change
- The books you read

Author and life coach Tony Fahkry says it well. "Life is a series of smaller destinations. The goal is to move from station to station." Said another way, the goal is to stay sober from meeting to meeting. Achieve small goals, such as working a Step, attending a group, reading a book. Don't put pressure on yourself to arrive, but to keep walking.

After my heart surgery November 11, 2022, my cardiologist challenged me to walk 10,000 steps every day. That translates to 1,752 miles per year. But I could never do that. What I can do is 10,000 steps today. It's about the journey – in life and in recovery.

RULE #88

If you want to go fast, go alone; if you want to go far, go together.

"Growth is never by mere chance; it is the result of forces working together."
J.C. Penny

What matters is not how fast you run, but how far you go. Some people treat recovery as a sprint. They race through the 12 Steps, read a new book every week, and attend a meeting every day. The problem is, they do it alone. Eventually, things come unraveled.

I read a great article by Greg Satell, "Why 'Move Fast and Break Things' Doesn't Work Anymore." The article is mostly about emerging technology, but Satell's broader point is that rushing through a project usually leaves us with disappointing results.

There are two ways to do recovery – fast and right. When you do recovery fast, you check boxes. The thinking is that we need to accomplish certain tasks in order to find recovery: (a) therapy, (b) group, (c) Step work, (d) amends, (e) spiritual disciplines, (f) more. We try to run through these so we can say, "Mission accomplished!" But here's what we miss. The opposite of addiction isn't sobriety; it's connection. Through connection, we achieve sobriety.

The other way to do recovery is together. We remember the Man Code. We have our 1 – God. We spend time with our 3 – inner circle. We embrace our 12 – small group. We attach to our 120 – church. And we reach out to our 5,000 – community. What we don't do is Lone Ranger recovery.

If you spend time with men and women with long-term sobriety, you will find a lot of differences among them. But there is one constant. They all do recovery within the context of community. That's what makes recovery groups so powerful. It doesn't really matter who is facilitating the group from week to week. The written material is good, but repetitious. The magic is in the connection.

So go ahead. You can run fast or you can run together. If long-term recovery is your goal, I suggest you run together.

RULE #89

You can't gain a year of sobriety in a day, but you can lose it in a day.

"I never planned a whole lot of future; it's one day at a time."
Darrell Royal

It takes 365 days of sobriety to gain a year. But it takes just one day of acting out to lose a year. Think about that the next time you are tempted to give in. Do you really want to reset your sobriety date? Do you want those who know you best to question your authenticity? Do you want to wake up tomorrow as Day 1, all over again?

I have told my wife many times, "I'm not saying I'll never act out again. I'm just saying it won't be today." I get a lot of criticism for that, but for me it works. I've learned to not make promises for days that God has not promised me. "Take no thought for tomorrow," the Bible says. Recovery is more of a "one-day-at-a-time" proposition than anything else in the world.

A good recovery plan addresses four questions:

- What will I do each day?
- What will I do each week?
- What will I do each month?
- What will I do each year?

The most important of those four questions (and it's not even close) is the first. What will I do each day? Writing for *Recovery International*, Ryan Michaels cites four benefits of a daily recovery routine.

- Routine keeps you busy.
- Routine gives you a sense of purpose.
- Routine allows you to replace bad habits with good ones.
- Routine keeps you accountable.

My advice is to forget about staying sober for the next year. Focus on the next day. Build in specific recovery routines for each day, habits that will be constant. Then, if you do recovery one day at a time, before you know it, the years will follow.

RULE #90

Recovery is hard. Regret is harder.

"It's better to look ahead and prepare,
than to look back and regret."
Jackie Joyner-Kersee

Life is full of regrets.

- Tina Turner: "I regret not having had more time with my kids when they were growing up."
- Nathan Hale: "I only regret that I have but one life to lose for my country."
- Jessica Lange: "I regret those times when I chose the dark side."
- Sylvester Stallone: "I have tons of regrets, but that's what pushes me."
- Yoko Ono: "The regret of my life is that I have not said 'I love you' often enough."
- Matt Lauer: "I regret the pain I've caused."
- J. Paul Getty: "I hate to be a failure. I regret the failure of my marriages. I would gladly give all my millions for just one lasting marital success."

Then there's this other regret I hear a lot. "I regret blowing up my sobriety for a moment of pleasure." I was in a large city recently, and wanted to take in a recovery meeting. I found one at a church, so I slipped in as the meeting was starting. During the check-in, the last person to speak was a young man who appeared to be less than 25 years of age. He stated his first name, and then he said something that has stuck with me. "Recovery is hard, but addiction is harder."

Yes, recovery is hard. But I'd add, regret is harder. It is hard to stay sober, do the work, and stick to my plan every single day. But recovery beats regret every day of the week. Let me ask you some questions.

- Would you rather do the work of recovery or experience the pain of regret?
- Have you ever regretted going to a recovery meeting?
- Have you ever regretted missing a recovery meeting?
- What does it feel like to look back at life with regrets?
- How hard are you willing to work on your recovery every day?

Yes, recovery is hard. It's *very hard* at times. But regret is so much harder. I know, because I've lived with both. I had years of regret and I have now had years of recovery. My biggest regret is not the things I did for so long, but the one thing I did not do for so long – recovery.

RULE #91

Never let a relapse go to waste.

"Part of recovery is relapse.
I dust myself off and move forward again."
Steven Adler

One of the foundational truths that has gotten me through some really hard times is this – what God allows, God redeems. Now, let's apply that to addiction relapse. God obviously allowed you to relapse, or it wouldn't have happened. While he didn't want it to happen, he allowed it to happen. And that puts you squarely in the "redemption zone." But in order for God to redeem your relapse, you have to do something first.

Perform an autopsy.

Take the time to ask yourself what was going on that led to your relapse. Addiction and relapse are not a bad problem as much as they are a bad solution. You relapsed for a reason. In order to do an autopsy on your relapse, in order to learn from it, ask yourself these questions.

- What was going on in the 24 hours leading up to my relapse?
- What was going on in the 24 minutes before the relapse?
- What did I fail to do that I could have done before the relapse?

- Was there a lapse in my self-care before the relapse?
- What can I do differently the next time I am triggered?
- Who will I tell about my relapse?
- What new guardrails can I put in place in the future?

Never take relapse lightly. David Sheff said, "Relapse is very dangerous. However, relapse can be a symptom of the disease. Sometimes there are multiple relapses before you get sober and stay sober." Underline that word – *sometimes*. There can be multiple relapses, but there doesn't have to be *any* relapses, from this moment forward.

When all else fails, remember that you can always say, "No." You will never act out against your will. Every relapse is the result of selfishness. The words of Paul still ring true. "With every temptation God gives a way to escape, that you might be able to escape" (1 Corinthians 10:13). You don't even need to pray for the strength to overcome. God has already given you that strength.

Freedom is a choice more than a condition. So when the next temptation hits, use every tool in your tool box – calls, 20-minute rule, thought replacement, and more. And then say, "No."

RULE #92

If you aren't in a 12-Step group, that might explain the mess you're in.

"It's simple, not necessarily easy, but the rewards are endless."
Anonymous Member, Narcotics Anonymous

If you are struggling to find traction in your recovery, and you are not in a recovery group, we may have found the problem. I'm not saying 12-Step groups are for everybody. But I am saying they have a pretty good history, stretching back to 1939. Until you find a better solution, you should give it a try. In 12-Step meetings, it is often said, "Give it six meetings." I agree with that. And the great thing is, in most areas, there are multiple groups to choose from.

When I got into recovery in 2013, there were 60 groups in my area, for my addiction. If you live away from large cities, you have the Zoom or phone-in options, as well. There really is no excuse to not find a group.

Having said that, there are plenty of other options that meet the same need. For example, I lead eight weekly groups for men who struggle with sexual addiction. I call them Freedom Groups. We use my 400-page workbook, *Life Recovery Plan*. The same book has been used to start other Freedom Groups around the U.S. and in Canada. While these are not 12-Step groups, we meet the same needs.

You might try Celebrate Recovery or some other Christ-centered group in your area, if you want a faith-based group. I suggest that you not be too picky. For my own recovery, I have attended "secular" 12-Step groups for ten years, as of this writing. I cringe when someone identifies his "higher power" as the group, or some other mystical deity. But that doesn't keep me from benefiting from the fellowship and stories in the room.

I will say this with confidence. If what you're doing is working, I like what you're doing. But if what you're doing isn't working, I don't like what you're doing. Have enough humility to admit your shortcomings and be open to the possibility that you just might not have all the answers.

There's another benefit of attending 12-Step meetings. You will meet one or two friends for life there. At this moment, I am writing this lesson while on a writing retreat at a really nice condo that is owned by a friend from my 12-Step group. He donated his place for the week. Now, I'm not promising a free condo if you join a 12-Step group, but I am promising you that you will establish relationships that will be with you and bless you for life. I'd say that 90 percent of my truly close friends are men I've met in recovery. The same can be true for you.

RULE #93

None of us has come so far that we can't fall, and none of us has come so short that we can't succeed.

"Anything and anyone can fail."
Frank Herbert

Did you see *Apollo 13*? When the spacecraft was in serious trouble, the Commander at the NASA mission control center said, "Failure is not an option." I've heard a lot of men and women in recovery say the same thing. "I've got this. I've come too far to fall. Failure is not an option."

And then they fell.

Let me remind you of a few of our previous Recovery Rules:

- No matter how far you go down the road of recovery, the ditch is still just as close on either side of the road.
- Freedom is a choice more than a condition.
- Past success is no guarantee of future results.

I would say that the bad news is that no matter how far you have come, you can still fall. But that's not bad news. It's good news! The fact that you can still fall is a gift, because that will keep driving you back to God and the things that got you this far in the first place. So praise God that you're not too big to fail!

The second part of this rule is just as critical. No one has such little sobriety that they can't succeed. Every person with five years, 10 years, and 20 years of sobriety has the same thing in common. For each of them, it all started with their first 24 hours.

We read this from Joyce E.A. Russell, the Dean of the Villanova School of Business: "You can't develop resilience with just success in your life. You have to experience setbacks in order to build resilience, but the good news is that your resilience gets stronger each time you overcome challenges or obstacles. But we have to understand what happened from our failure – reverse engineer it to see what we can learn from this experience."

So whether you have ten years of sobriety or ten minutes, remember that you can still fail. But you can also still make it – for the rest of your life. And you are the only one who gets to make that decision.

RULE #94

Never be a prisoner of your past. It was just a lesson, not a life sentence.

"Even a spineless anthropod sheds what's no longer useful and leaves it behind them. Are you not greater than they?"
Jason Versey

What the spineless anthropod can do, you can do better! Shed what is no longer useful and leave it behind you! As Elsa said in *Frozen*, as an expression of her liberation, "Let it go! Let it go!" That would be a great affirmation for you to repeat at the start of every day: "Let it go! Let it go!"

When you see your past trauma, abuse, and isolation as a life sentence, rather than a lesson, you get stuck. And that's never a good place to be. When we make the pain of years gone by our main focus, we keep recreating our past into our future. I'm not saying you can forget your past, or that you even should if that was possible. It's okay to visit your past from time to time. But don't live there.

Dr. Jennice Vilhauer is the developer of Future Directed Therapy, as well as the director of the Outpatient Psychotherapy Treatment Program at Emory Healthcare. Her message to her patients is summed up with two words – "living forward." Dr. Vilhauer suggests three steps to breaking free from our past.

Step 1 – Notice that you are expecting something negative or unwanted to occur. The way you do this is by observing your emotions. If you are expecting something positive, you will be feeling good about it. But if you are expecting something unwanted, it will be marked by a negative emotion such as anxiety, fear, or hopelessness.

Step 2 – If you are sensing negative expectations, ask yourself, "What do I want instead?" This will help you to identify a different outcome to work toward. As an example, if you are dreading an upcoming party, redefine your expectations by turning them positive. State your preferred outcome.

Step 3 – Having defined your preferred outcome, ask a final question. "How do I make this happen?" When you do this, you are engaging the part of your brain known as the executive network, which can help you find ideas and solutions that will give you the results you need. This will complete your 180-degree turn from the negative to the positive.

RULE #95

The game is never won or lost at halftime.

"Never give up at halftime.
Concentrate on winning the second half."
Bear Bryant

Years ago, in my first pastorate (1984-2001), we had a young couple with whom we grew very close. The wife was (and still is) an accomplished banker. Naturally, we put her to work on important committees and projects. After observing my leadership for several years, she made a constructive comment that I have never forgotten. "You're a better starter than you are a finisher."

We stay in contact with these friends, even though we moved away decades ago. Last year, we gathered for dinner, and I thanked her for that observation from so many years ago. She didn't even remember telling me this, but I'm so glad she did. I often play those words forward, because they are still true. The way I'm wired, my satisfaction is in starting projects, much more than finishing them. I get that from Dad, the first entrepreneur I ever knew.

But in recovery, it's all about finishing strong. J.I. Packer observed, "Runners in a distance race always try to keep something in reserve for a final sprint." That's good advice for recovery. Always have something in front of you for which you are striving.

King Asa ruled Judah for an impressive 41 years. Asa "did what was right in the eyes of the Lord" (1 Kings 15:11). Good man, that Asa! By walking with God, he conquered the Ethiopian army (2 Chronicles 14:12). He enacted significant religious reforms (2 Chronicles 14:3-4). He did other great things, but all of this was during the first 36 years of his reign.

Then the wheels came off. Nearly 90 percent of the way through his reign, he got crosswise with Israel's king, Baasha. He made a series of poor judgments, quit relying on God, and did things his own way. The results were catastrophic.

What King Asa started, he did not finish. That leaves him on the scrap heap of failed kings. The same is true for too many of us. A good start does not guarantee a good finish. But the opposite is also true. You may be trailing at halftime, but with God as your quarterback, a comeback is in the works. So keep playing. Just remember to let him call the plays.

RULE #96

Recovery is never owned. It is rented. And payment is due every day.

"There is power in the daily schedule."
Gateway Foundation

"Mission accomplished." Those are two words my wife will never hear me say. I'd like to be able to say them, but as long as I'm in a daily fight for recovery, I can say I'm winning, but not that I've won. Recovery is never owned. It is rented. And payment is due every day. This requires focus and consistency.

Let's talk about three techniques for maintaining success in your recovery. These principles are borrowed from Laura Berger and Glen Tibaldeo, the authors of *Radical Sabbatical*, written to help people build the tenacity that is required to maintain permanent life change.

The first thing you need to do is write down your specific recovery goals. A poor example of what this might look like: "I plan to stay sober for the next 12 months." Here's a better way to say it: "For the next 24 hours, I will abstain from all drugs and alcohol. Then I will do that the next day. My goal is to string together 365 days of total abstinence." Another good statement might be, "I will not look at any pornographic images." Or, "I will stay off all social media for the next seven days."

Second, prioritize your tasks. This requires a specific, step-by-step recovery plan. Include recovery meetings you will attend. Write down the names of the people you will call to stay accountable. Determine your plan for recovery work, literature you will read, and other work you will do. Order these tasks in order of importance.

Finally, create balance. Think of it like this – all work is recovery work. By that, I mean, what you do in terms of exercise, spiritual disciplines, social interactions, your vocational work – it all affects your sobriety. Here are a few things you need to do, that you might not think really matter:

- Daily exercise
- Walks in nature
- Calls to an old friend
- Therapist sessions
- Check-ins with spouse

Find ways to make payments on your recovery every day. Think beyond the "big stuff," like meetings and extended therapy. Focus on the "little stuff" that you can do every day.

RULE #97

To choose addiction over sobriety is like eating out of a dumpster with a supermarket next door.

"I've come to give you life more abundantly."
Jesus

The story is told about a man who desperately wanted to take a trip from America to Europe by boat. He saved his money until he had just enough to pay the fare. But then it occurred to him that he'd need a little more money, to cover the cost of food for the voyage. This was a long time ago, when it took a month to cross the Atlantic. So he bought the cheapest food that would sustain him that long – a barrel of crackers and cheese.

For the first couple of weeks on the trip, he could tolerate his crackers and cheese, three times a day. But by the third and fourth weeks, it became really hard, especially as the man smelled the aroma of grilled steaks and other fine foods that the other passengers were enjoying.

During the final week, he couldn't take it anymore. So he jumped a guy walking by with a steak and begged him for the food. The other guy asked him if he had a ticket for the voyage. The man said, "Of course I do!" The other guy said, "Take out your ticket and read it."

When the man pulled his ticket out of his pocket, he saw something he had somehow missed when he bought it. The ticket read, "Meals included."

Quit eating crackers and cheese when meals are included! And quit thinking in terms of where you are headed, and enjoy the voyage. Jesus said that he came to give us life. But not just life. Life more abundantly. Translation – quit eating out of the dumpster when the supermarket is just a few feet away.

Recovery should be fun. Go to meetings early and hang out with the gang. Meet one of them for dinner or lunch. Find a new hobby that brings great enjoyment. Practice healthy self-care that brings joy and laughter. Enjoy the journey. You deserve the supermarket; otherwise, Jesus wouldn't have died on the cross.

Keep your eyes on the prize. Let your destination always be on your mind. But don't forget to enjoy the journey. And remember – meals included.

RULE #98

When you act out to "get it out of your system," you are really getting it into your system.

"You better get that out of your system, 'cause in two hours, you're gonna be Mrs. Anthony Lombardo."
Modern Family, 2009

"Just one more time." Have you ever said that? I know I said it – a lot. There is a saying in recovery groups that goes like this: "The only way we knew to be free of it was to do it." Call it one last fling. Or one more drink. The delusion plays out every day for millions of addicts. "I'm just doing this one more time so I can get it out of my system." And we actually believe that. The problem is, it doesn't work. By taking in the drink or image, we are really getting it *into* our system. We are creating new images and memories to add to our stockpile, which will make sobriety tomorrow just that much harder.

Timmen L. Cermak is a psychiatrist who specializes in addiction medicine, and has written several books on the subject. He says that several things happen when we indulge our addiction.

- Substance and behavioral addictions distort the personality of the person indulging.

- By doing it "one more time," the effects become self-centeredness, irresponsibility, and blaming others.
- Family members harden their hearts from the repeated behaviors.

Dr. Cermak concludes, "A brain hijacked by addiction loses all perspective."

From my experience, men and women who give in to a "final indulgence" are generally sincere. That's hard for the non-addict to comprehend. But what makes no sense to the sober mind makes perfect sense to the addict. You have heard, "The definition of insanity is doing the same thing over and over, expecting different results." You could switch out "addiction" for "insanity" and still be correct.

The definition of *addiction* is doing the same thing over and over, expecting different results. In the addict's mind, one more indulgence will satisfy. One more sexual encounter or porn image. One more roll of the dice. One more drink. One more pill. Just one more. That's all it will take. But remember, one is too many and a thousand is never enough.

But take heart. There is a way to get it out of your system. Quit putting it into your system! No more liquor. No more pills. No more porn. No more whatever. Starve the beast. Eventually, this will rewire your brain. And tomorrow will thank you for that.

RULE #99

Your past explains your addictive behaviors, but it doesn't excuse your addictive behaviors.

"He who is good for making excuses
is seldom good for anything else."
Benjamin Franklin

As a recovering addict myself, I am sympathetic to the plight of other addicts. I'm sensitive to the fact that no one wants to be here. No one asks for their addiction. I have created a model that I call the "addiction pyramid." At the top of the pyramid are the acting out behaviors. The second tier of the pyramid consists of the five primary triggers that make us the most vulnerable – when we are bored, lonely, angry, stressed, or tired.

The third layer of the pyramid is whatever feeds the triggers. And beneath the surface is the bottom tier, which generally includes trauma, abuse, and isolation. This model serves to explain how we got here. But this is the inconvenient truth – *every time you act out, that's on you*.

While some people have a much more difficult path to sobriety than others, they still have a choice, every time they are triggered. Their past explains a lot, but it excuses nothing.

Tim Pychyl, retired professor at Carleton University, has produced what he calls the "hierarchy of excuses." He contends that our tendency is to take the path of least resistance. This hierarchy lists four responses to our triggers, from the most preferred to the least. Keep in mind, this is not the best way to respond, but is an explanation of the addict's irresponsible excuse-making.

1. Rationalize our behaviors – justify the acting out.
2. Deny responsibility for our behavior – blame others.
3. Distract ourselves from the dissonance itself – a form of denial.
4. Change our behavior – the last thing the addict wants to do.

The first thing you must do to overcome your addiction is to own it. That is Step 1 – admit that you have a problem and are powerless to do anything about it. This is the only Step you must work perfectly. It is a matter of exchanging a comma for a period. Too often, early in our recovery, we disclose, "I have been viewing porn, but you need to understand the way I was raised." Or, "Yes, I've hidden liquor in my office, but I never would have taken my first drink if my brother had not given me a beer when I was 13 years old."

Anytime there is a comma, we are just making excuses. If I'm going to be serious about recovery, I must first be serious about my addiction. No commas. "I have a drinking problem – *period.*" "I gamble too much – *period.*" "I have had multiple affairs – *period.*" "I have hidden cash – *period.*" "I have a food addiction – *period.*" "No excuses, it's on me. I am taking ownership for my disease so I can take responsibility for my recovery."

RULE #100

Rock bottom is a great foundation on which to build.

"I hit rock bottom, but thank God my bottom wasn't death."
Stevie Ray Vaughan

Is it necessary to hit bottom in order to find recovery? Absolutely not! God will take you wherever you are. He's not waiting around for you to completely blow up your marriage, become homeless, lose all your friends, and contract a life-threatening disease in order to hear your prayers. Feel free to repent, to seek God, and to get into recovery anytime. No need to wait. Having said that, by an overwhelming percent, most addicts fail to get help until their addiction really costs them something. That's the nature of addiction. That's the nature of sin. And that's the nature of man.

For most of us, we didn't get into recovery until a significant setback of some kind. In the 14th century, Italian poet Dante Alighieri wrote the famous work, *Divine Comedy*. Within the poem we read this line – "The path to paradise begins in hell." That is true for most of us; we hit rock bottom before we get serious. Hitting rock bottom is when a person feels emotionally overwhelmed and broken. They will frequently feel flattened with hardly any energy. Hitting rock bottom is accompanied with a feeling of absolute terror and desperation.

Author Michael Meade writes, "Until people realize what harms them and limits them from within, they are unlikely to call out for someone to help stop the pain." And Rod Judkins, who writes on the ingredients of change, adds, "When someone hits rock bottom, there's no lower place to go. Hitting the bottom is so painful that it's enough to motivate a person to recovery."

Let's consider a few questions that will help you see where you are in the process.

1. Has your addiction cost you anything?
2. Have you hit your rock bottom?
3. How desperate are you to get well?
4. What are you willing to do to get well?
5. Is there anything you are not willing to do to find sobriety?
6. How soon will you get to a recovery meeting?
7. Are you ready to break up with your most reliable friend – your addiction?

I wouldn't wish the pain that comes with hitting rock bottom on my worst enemy. But I do pray for what comes with that. Rock bottom is a tough pill to swallow, but for most of us, it was the only medicine that worked. Why would God allow you to hit bottom? Because God allows what he hates in order to do what he loves. He loves you too much to leave you to your addiction. If you have to hit rock bottom in order to get well, that is not a price too high.

CONCLUSION

There are hundreds of addictions. Most of us have more than one. But we are really all in the same boat. Wherever your addiction has taken you, the way out is the same for everybody. I encourage you to go to any means necessary to get help. Join a group. See a therapist. Work the Steps. Improve your spiritual disciplines. Become accountable. Practice self-care.

Recovery is for life. Until your addiction takes a day off, your recovery should stay alert. If you do the work, put in the time, and go all in, good things will happen. I know, because it worked for me. And if this book of Rules has been helpful to you, great! Our purpose was to provide a simple supplement to your regular recovery regimen. This is no substitute for your other work. But hopefully, you have found this useful.

This book is really still being written – by you. Come up with your own Recovery Rules. I love to steal the ideas of others, so feel free to shoot me an email. Let me know your Rules. Who knows? Maybe there will be a second volume out there somewhere.

I want you to know that you are not alone. We aren't the only ministry addressing the pandemic of addiction. Reach out, if not to us, to someone. You can win this battle, but you can't do it alone.

This has been a fun journey for me. I am grateful that you joined me along the way. My prayer is that you will take the most important step in your recovery.

The next step . . .

www.ingramcontent.com/pod-product-compliance
Lightning Source LLC
Chambersburg PA
CBHW071933090426
42740CB00011B/1692